# Also available at all good book stores

9781785316470

9781785313929

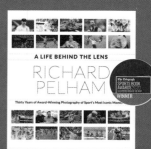

9781785315466

9781785316487

9781785316708

9781785316814

9781785317286

9781785316838

9781785315381

# GENERAZIONE WUNDERTEAM

# GENERAZIONE
# WUNDERTEAM

## THE RISE AND FALL OF
## AUSTRIA'S WONDER TEAM

### JO ARAF

Originally published in Italy by Urbone Publishing

This edition published by Pitch Publishing, 2021

Pitch Publishing
A2 Yeoman Gate
Yeoman Way
Worthing
Sussex
BN13 3QZ
www.pitchpublishing.co.uk
info@pitchpublishing.co.uk

A CIP catalogue record is available for this book
from the British Library.

ISBN 978-1 78531 852 8

Typesetting and origination by Pitch Publishing
Printed and bound in India by Replika Press Pvt. Ltd.

# CONTENTS

*To my parents*

# INTRODUCTION

WHEN WEST Germany and Austria faced each other during the 1978 World Cup, the Austrian fans exploded with joy at the final whistle of the Israeli referee Klein. Their countrymen had prevailed in what had become Austria's most important international derby since the end of the Second World War. Austria, however, had arrived at the match without any chance of progression: they had already been eliminated by virtue of previous matches, but a victory against their historic rival gave a World Cup that ended prematurely some form of achievement. Not least because Austria were not a bad team: Herbert Prohaska, Hans Krankl and Walter Schachner among others were in a very respectable squad.

That victory, although useless, was acclaimed by all and later remembered as the 'Miracle of Cordoba'. To speak of a 'miracle' in relation to a defeat might seem a paradox, especially in view of the fact that Germany, after winning the World Cup in 1954 against Hungary, had renamed that sporting feat the 'Miracle of Bern'. Moreover, although the Austrian national team in 1978 was not one of the world leaders, it boasted a tradition that most other sides could only take their hats off to. In 1954 Austria had finished third in the World Cup, and several years before the outbreak of the Second World War they had won the International Cup, a forerunner of the modern European Championships. They had been among the favourites for the 1934 World Cup, the second playing of the tournament but the first that Austria took part in. What made the Austrian line-up so popular was the *Scheiberlspiel,* a style of play made up of short passes and ball possession that the coach of the Austrians, Hugo Meisl, had developed and perfected over the previous 20 years.

Starting in 1931, the Austrian national team would become the Wunderteam for everyone. When they didn't win they were booed; when they did win they were convincing. On one occasion – an unenthusiastic victory against Switzerland – the press were dissatisfied with a triumph called 'an insufficient show for 55,000 people'. Austria's fans had developed a taste for football on a par with Vienna's taste for the arts and literature. Austrian players were asked to perform in a sporting spectacle where the result would be secondary to the performance and entertainment that ensued, just like when the Viennese went to the cinema to see a film directed by Fritz Lang or attended an exhibition by Oskar Kokoschka.

But how did a national team like Austria make their mark on the most important stage of the time and earn a reputation as the world's best trainers, so much so that they were renamed the Wunderteam?

To figure that out, you have to take a few steps back. The story goes back to the founding fathers, the English, and their rival football philosophy from Scotland. Within the then Austro-Hungarian Empire it was the Scottish school that would prevail thanks to the arrival in Austria, Hungary and Czechoslovakia of Scottish or English players and coaches who had repudiated their school in favour of their opposite. The result was a style of play that would go down in international history as a 'Central European School', although the first to be fascinated were the Italians who renamed the newborn 'Danube football' movement. Danubian football was based on a key idea: the ball had to run and not the players. In England such a system had only taken root in very few cases, and there was a strong feeling of how Austria, who would reach their football peak in the early 1930s, would be able to put England in the shadows thanks to the weapons that the British themselves had provided.

As per tradition, in 1932 – a few months after the Wunderteam had won the International Cup – Austria were invited to England, as the strongest team on the continent, for a friendly match. And as tradition had it, the English had arraanged the friendly in the winter period, so that the playing field was more suited to their style. Austria lost, but both the English and Austrian newspapers spared no praise for the formation coached by Hugo Meisl.

But it was not only the technique of its interpreters and a refined style of play that made training cutting-edge: in the years between the two wars, Austria faced high unemployment and continuous lay-offs along with perpetual political instability. Football had become a distraction from the daily routine, and by 1924 it had become a source of income for players thanks to the efforts of Meisl, who had made the Austrian league a professional one. The same evolution would be observed within two years in Czechoslovakia and Hungary, two other countries that emerged with broken bones from the First World War and had suffered as much as Austria.

# I

# AT THE ROOTS OF THE WUNDERTEAM: THE BIRTH OF DANUBIAN FOOTBALL

*Within the Austro-Hungarian Empire – which stretched over an area of about 70,000km² and included, among others, present-day Austria, Hungary and the Czech Republic – frequent invectives were directed from Vienna to its Hungarian neighbours. The dominant thought among the upper classes of Viennese society was that Budapest was a sort of younger sister of Vienna, poorer and backward. This stereotypical and derogatory view was summed up in the words of the politician and traveller Francz Von Löher, 'There is no cultural idea, neither of a legal, military, state, religious, social, artistic or scientific nature, nor of any other field from Hungary that has spread to the civilised world.' The truth is that the Hungarians have remained the same commercially as they were a thousand years ago, when their camps stood out along the Asian steppes. Austrian anti-Semites, moreover, used to refer to Budapest as 'Judapest', claiming it was 'a city of gypsies and Jews'. The then*

*Czechoslovakia and the Bohemian and Moravian economic migrants who had settled in the suburbs of Vienna were also targeted. Karl Lueger, mayor of Vienna, Hitler's inspirer and creator of the Christian Social Party, in reference to the migration flows from Bohemia and Moravia said, 'Vienna must continue to be Germanic and the Germanic character of the city must not be questioned.' In 1897, the founding of the Challenge Cup was to re-propose these bitter rivalries for the first time in football.*

1

FOOTBALL IN Austria was developed on the English model in the last years of the 19th century and spread from some elite circles in Vienna. The spread was progressive and involved suburbs, smaller cities and rural areas. The growth of other sports alongside football included disciplines such as horse riding – galloping had appeared in 1839 and trotting in 1878 – gymnastics, running and the notorious Viennese ice skating school. Later, alpine sports, climbing, cycling, athletics and grass tennis would also became popular.

But within a few years football had reached peaks of popularity never seen before, thanks to its ability to spread in Vienna first and, later, within the whole country. If before the Great War sport had been almost exclusively for the aristocracy and bourgeoisie, with the advent of the conflict it began to take root at the front and in the prison camps as a pastime among soldiers. With the end of hostilities and the birth of the First Austrian Republic, it became one of the activities through which men at labour camps used to spend their free time.

Thanks to new laws that allowed workers more flexible hours and a shorter working day, an increasing number of sports clubs emerged in the cities and suburbs. The interest of the population in sport had been strengthened by the war experience: the desire and opportunity to dedicate oneself to recreational and sporting activities in groups had never been shared as much as in the years following the Great War. And it was thanks to sport that a climate of solidarity and a sense of community, accompanied by participation in various disciplines, was generated both in bourgeois circles and in factory environments. It was precisely in this context that in 1931 Vienna would organise the second edition of the Olympic Games of the Workers.

The birth of Viennese football was the work of the English founding fathers. They were the first to play football in the Austrian capital and were employees of several British companies based in Vienna. The key year was 1894: First Vienna and Vienna Cricket and Football Club were born almost simultaneously. One of the main differences between the two was that while Vienna Cricket and Football Club had only English players, First Vienna was also open to non-British players: in 1897, in the 11 of First Vienna there were five Austrian players, although there was also the English-speaking John Mac and another player had joined the team after experience in England.

Between 1897 and 1900 there were 45 clubs in the capital, 17 of which joined the ÖFU, the Austrian Football Union, the first football association founded in Austria, in 1900. The ÖFU was dissolved only four years later, however, when First Vienna and Vienna Cricket and Football Clubs, following some differences, founded the ÖFV, which only a year later would join FIFA. But from 1926, two years after the turning point towards professional football, the ÖFV was replaced by the ÖFB. However, the differences between the two would be minimal and purely organisational in nature.

The initial function of football was mainly to involve English immigrants in an outside-of-work activity aimed at occupying their leisure time. After a few years, however, the increased interest in the world of football grew, even in the newspapers that dedicated more and more ink to matches. In 1897, John Gramlick, a leading member of Vienna Cricket and Football Club, founded the first international club competition in which all the formations of the Austro-Hungarian Empire could take part, the Challenge Cup (or Challenge Kupa, as it was called in Budapest). Between 1899 and 1910, other important clubs such as Rapid Vienna, Admira and Wacker were born.

The English imprint was also immediately evident in the terms adopted about roles, such as goalkeeper, centre-back, half-back, forward and other football-related terms such as cup, penalty or derby.

In the years to come, the union between football and England within the Austrian capital was further strengthened thanks to some English players who had emigrated to Vienna over the years to work for British clubs. One example was that of Magnus Douglas Nicholson, a player from West Bromwich Albion who moved to Vienna on business – he worked for the Thomas Cook travel agency, became a First Vienna player and began to promote football by organising tours for English teams in the Austrian capital.

A small audience of fans was created among the Viennese bourgeoisie, and ticket prices were deliberately kept high in order to keep the proletarian classes at bay and to ensure that football retained an elitist matrix. As in other countries, Austrian football owed a great deal to the English founding fathers, including some founding characteristics such as club names, an emphasis on fair play, in some cases playing styles and slang borrowed from the English language. These elements distinguished the beginnings of Viennese football and in some cases have survived to the present day.

Over the years, however, the practice of football began to spread to other segments of the population: it became fashionable to play in the streets, parks and squares of Vienna. Any object with a round shape could take the place of a ball if necessary. Players and spectators from the suburbs and working classes began to increase in number and the style of play that had developed in those years was transformed. Victory began to be considered more important than fair play and mere participation, and towards the end of the First World War Viennese football had definitely become the pastime and sport of the proletariat. Spectator numbers had increased considerably and many clubs had begun to flourish, especially within the capital. One of the main differences in the enjoyment of sport between workers and the bourgeois classes was their ultimate goal: among the workers, the main objective was recreation and distraction from the working routine, while within the bourgeois circles more emphasis was placed on results and the consequent economic gains.

Even the facilities had been redesigned from the early years: now several stadiums were able to accommodate 70,000 or 80,000 spectators, a sign that football had become a mass phenomenon. In the space of a few years, the social impact of football would have reached that of cinema, surpassing art, music and literature, which, compared to the game of football, did not make an impact on an equally large and heterogeneous audience. 'Daddy's beer, Mummy's cinema and brother's football,' it was said in Vienna.

Thus was born in the early 1920s a deep-rooted football culture around the Austrian capital, characterised by the ability to mobilise the masses and to represent almost exclusively a male phenomenon, although some women's clubs had appeared after 1918. It was a culture largely confined to the capital, and at the highest levels things would remain unchanged until the end of the Second World War. The same phenomenon had occurred in Prague and Budapest, which, like Vienna, monopolised the national football scene. Thus was born what was later called the Central European School, which in the 1920s, '30s and '40s would churn out several of the greatest champions of the time.

Shortly after the end of the Great War, football in Vienna had become a mass spectator sport. In previous years, stadium attendance hardly exceeded 10,000, even when Austria were facing their great rivals, Hungary. And since the end of the war, a new type of fan had appeared: the suburban fan, usually belonging to the proletarian class. The aggressive behaviour of these supporters was initially motivated – according to the chronicles of the time – by the bitterness of the defeat suffered in the Great War and the repercussions that had mainly affected the suburbs. The *Neues Wiener Journal* wrote about this in 1922, 'Since then – since the end of the Great War – the riots caused by the crowds have not only increased, but have also grown in violence. Fans are now used to carrying wooden clubs and stones, and when hordes from Fuchsen or Drachenfeld [at the time the most infamous districts on the outskirts of Vienna] flock to the matches, it is not uncommon to see stabbings.'

But it was in the very suburbs where hunger dominated that football began to sprout. Most of the fans and players came from Fuchsen, Drachenfeld, Ottakring, Favoriten and other areas of the capital, and the main sports facilities were almost all located outside the city centre.

The clubs were almost all characterised by a social and sporting identity: there was the elite and bourgeois club, Austria Vienna, and proletarian clubs such as Rapid as well as, of course, apolitical teams and sports clubs that rejected any kind of label. In the early years, Austria Vienna and Rapid enjoyed the greatest popularity, as evidenced by the number of spectators attending their home matches.

In 1924 the Austrian professional championship was born and officially began on 21 September of that year. And from the early 1930s, Austrian – or rather Viennese – football entered its heyday thanks to the successes of the Wunderteam and the victories of Austrian clubs in the newly founded Mitropa Cup, the highest European competition for club teams, which was founded in 1927.

The fact that the Austrian championship had become professional, however, had entailed burdens and honours: those unable to stay afloat financially had to reluctantly accept participation in minor tournaments.

On average, 40,000 people were in attendance to see the Wunderteam, Austria Vienna or Rapid play. Football had become a business in its own right, and several companies were beginning to associate their products with the most famous faces of the game.

After the Great War, football also represented the main international showcase of a city whose charm as a European metropolis had faded considerably. The Viennese School remained famous throughout the world and this halo of popularity also benefited the smaller teams, who were often invited to play friendly matches in other European countries. Austrian players and coaches were also regularly contracted by foreign clubs. An article from 1924 entitled 'Europe's football capital, Vienna, is still in the lead' said, 'Vienna is the capital of the European continent. Where else can you see at least 40,000–50,000 spectators gather Sunday after Sunday at any stadium, even when it rains? In what other city is the majority of the population so interested in the results of the matches that in the evening almost everyone discusses the championship, the prospects of their club and subsequent matches?'

As Austrian football was an almost exclusively Viennese phenomenon, the capital's clubs found that their most bitter rivals were not from the neighbouring city, but the big teams from their own city or the best European teams they clashed with in the Mitropa Cup: Bologna, Ambrosiana, Juventus and the teams from Budapest, Berlin and Prague. In the cosmopolitan Vienna of the time, one of the city's main institutions, the coffee houses, became the places where discussions between fans took place.

And just as coffee houses had contributed to the hunger of artists and writers, the same thing happened with football stars. Later on, as several exponents of the then Austrian modernism admitted, the Wunderteam's exploits during the '30s would become one of the most discussed topics. Rooted in each neighbourhood, coffee houses often reflected the cultural and linguistic identity of their area. They spread throughout the country towards the end of the Habsburg Empire and were the places where men and women from all walks of life met, despite the fact that coffee houses were made famous by the presence of bohemians and personalities from the most famous literary circles. They were not simply places where people sat and chatted over a cup of coffee. It was possible to find newspapers, which otherwise was not simply because there were not many kiosks in town to sell them. And the more regular customers – called Stammgäste – could also receive mail or wash their clothes. Card games and chess challenges were the order of the day, as was the organisation of pre-election meetings.

Since the 1920s, when football began to take root and the first professional league championship saw the light, something new appeared on the Viennese scene: the coffee houses of the football teams.

The supporters of Austria Vienna found themselves at Café Parsifal, right in the centre, while those of Rapid used to go to Café Holub, owned by Johann Holub, president of the club for 11 years, on Hütteldorferstrasse, where they also had their playing field. Café Resch in the Meidling district was the main meeting place for Wacker fans while Simmering fans gathered at a coffee house owned by their most prominent player, Johann Horvath. There were also more inclusive coffee houses, where fans from different teams would talk about football. One of the most famous was undoubtedly the Café Ring, which began as a meeting place for the English-speaking cricket community but soon became a favourite haunt for football fans. It was a place where anyone could say their piece about victories, defeats, transfers, national team matches or foreign tours for their club. Café Ring was defined as 'a kind of revolutionary parliament of friends and football fanatics'. One of Café Ring's most frequent visitors was undoubtedly Wunderteam coach Hugo Meisl.

Under the aegis of Austro-Fascism beforehand and German National Socialism afterwards, football would remain a means of expressing a national consciousness. It wasn't until 1942 that the turmoil around the world meant football suffered an abrupt setback due to the summons to the battlefront of most of the players taking part in the championship.

The *Scheiberlspiel* was born, a style of play that reflected a mentality focused on technique, cunning and the development of an approach where the collective took precedence over the individual. In addition, during the inter-war period in Austria unemployment had exploded, and becoming a footballer was undoubtedly a way of escaping poverty and ensuring a survival anchor for oneself and one's family.

The beginning of the 1938 football season coincided with the entry of German troops into Vienna, and the Austrian

*Scheiberlspiel* began to have to deal with a style of play that was in many ways antithetical – the German style – based on physical and moral exercise and strongly imbued with military aspects. According to the German school, a football team had first of all to be 'ready to fight'.

# 2

THERE ARE several historical interpretations of the appearance of football in Hungary, although they all seem to date back to the last years of the 19th century, when football appeared on the sports scene in Vienna and Prague.

A first hypothesis maintains that the inauguration of Hungarian football would be due to Károly Löwenrosen, a Hungarian citizen who, after an experience in England, would return home with a ball that he presented at the Millennial Exhibition. Another theory attributes the merits to László Kosztovics. According to this version, it was Kosztovics, a student, who spread football in Hungary in 1879, although his initial attempt to promote it in the town of Szentendre, north of Budapest and along the banks of the Danube, was not very successful. A third theory sees Miksa Eszterházy, an important diplomat and landowner during the Austro-Hungarian Empire, as the importer of football in the Hungarian capital around 1875.

To this day, no one knows for sure where the truth lies. What is clear, however, is that football had developed in Budapest in the second half of the 19th century, from 1875 onwards. And we also know with certainty the year in which the first team, BTC – Budapest Torna Club – was born, 1897. A few months later, football would have spread from the cities to the provinces and withiny existing sports clubs.

From 1880 onwards, several associations had blossomed in the form of multi-sports clubs with a local, social or ethnic-religious character. The UTE – Újpesti Torna Egylet – the Gymnastics Club of Újpest, and the BTC – Budapest Torna Club – were born.

From the NTE, another sports club composed of members of the Jewish bourgeoisie who considered gymnastics too conservative, MTK – Magyar Testgyakorlók Köre – the Hungarian Circle of Body Instructors, was born in 1888. The term Circle appeared for the first time instead of 'Club' or 'Association', which were considered too elitist or conservative respectively. Despite the Jewish matrix of the club, the founders of MTK had been motivated more by practical principles than ideologies, and from the very beginning their mission had been to create 'a place where anyone, without discrimination, could take part in the "newest" sports at the highest level'. This referred to the disciplines covered by the newborn multi-sports club that included football and excluded those classically practiced by the aristocracy, which did not allow Jews to participate in activities such as fencing or horse riding.

But beyond the image that the founders had tried to convey to the outside world, the local public would identify the two most important clubs in the city, MTK and FTC (Ferencvárosi Torna Club), founded in 1899, with two distinct labels: MTK would become the Jewish club for everyone, and Ferencváros the club of German origin, born 11 years after MTK in the ninth district of Budapest. Several clubs began to flourish around the cities, districts and neighbourhoods of the country, giving rise to an initial geographical distinction. In 1901, the Magyar Labdarúgó Szövetség (MLSZ), the Hungarian Football Federation, was founded.

Compared to the sports traditionally practiced by the aristocratic classes, football was characterised by some new elements such as contact and physical confrontation. In 1900, a 'friendly' between the Berliners and the Hungarian Athletics Club raised more than one concern as several players reported injuries. This led Ágoston Del Medico, a member of the city council, to propose the suppression of football in all schools in the country. Many schools supported this motion, although an assembly in 1900 declared in favour of the survival of the game.

From 1901, football would be universally accepted or, in any case, would no longer have to fight for its right to exist. Only two months earlier, a league had also been set up, bringing together Hungarian formations – or rather, the capital's formations – around the traditional rules of English football. Hungarian football – as had happened in Vienna – also borrowed some terms from the English founding fathers, such as football, replaced over the years by its Hungarian translation 'labdarúgás'. From the 1906/07 season the championship would be played in autumn and winter, which was more suited to central European weather conditions. If the first two championships went to the BTC, the oldest team in the country, from 1903 a dualism began that would rage for the next 26 years: during this period, interspersed with the events of war, no other club except MTK and Fradi, the name by which we still refer to Ferencváros, would win any title. Fradi, moreover, was the only Hungarian club to triumph in the short history of the Challenge Cup. This duopoly was interrupted by Újpest in the 1929/30 season.

At first, the differentiation between the clubs also concerned the different styles of play: BTC practised the so-called kick and rush borrowed from the English masters, by virtue of the physicality of their players who came from the world of gymnastics and whose technique lent itself to wide margins of improvement; FTC did not deviate much.

They played a kick and rush seasoned with sporadic and fine dribbling and head shots; MTK for their part had adopted the Scottish philosophy of passing from the back. To preserve this attitude to technique in spite of the physicality and roughness of their opponents, the then president Alfréd Brüll hired a Scottish player, Edward Shires, and two of his countrymen as coaches between 1911 and 1914: John Tait Robertson and James 'Jimmy' Hogan, who more than anyone else contributed to the Scottish flavour in the history of the club. Gusztáv Sebes, future coach of Aranycsapat – the great Hungarian national team in which he played with Puskás and who reached the World Cup Final in 1954 – said of Hogan, 'We play football as Hogan taught us. His name should be written in gold letters every time the history of our football is written.' The end of the war coincided with the collapse of several clubs because of the ensuing economic and political disasters.

One of the ways in which clubs' finances were tried to balance out was the 'ball-attrition fee', a tax that the visiting side paid to the home team for the mere use of the ball. It was also a phase during which, again due to the devastating economic situation, many players left Hungary to settle elsewhere, such as in Germany, where, although only for a few years, a team composed solely of Hungarian players would be formed.

What slowed the first important wave of Hungarian players moving to other shores – the second one would arrive around 1956 with the outbreak of the Hungarian Revolution – was the creation of a professional league for the 1926/27 season, in the footsteps of what had happened in Austria and Czechoslovakia in the two previous years. This brought advantages such as greater care of the youth sectors, an improvement in the preparation of coaches and referees and a strengthening of international relations between national selections and club teams from different countries. In addition, the tours of Hungarian teams to other countries in Europe – and even overseas – became frequent: FTC, for example, defeated Uruguay away from home in 1929, Újpest won in Geneva a year later and MTK, then Hungária, played matches in Egypt, Mexico and the United States in 1934. Touring became such an established practice that it even went so far as to adversely affect players' performance both nationally and internationally. Often, during matches, the players seemed visibly worn out by their foreign commitments and for this reason in 1935 it was decided to merge the professional and amateur leagues. This move was the basis for the creation of a generation of competitive champions who would reach the World Cup Final in 1938.

During its first 24 years of history, the Hungarian championship had remained reserved for teams from the capital, and only in the 1925/26 season did a provincial team, Erzsébetfalvi TC, appear for the first time. From then on, the presence of clubs from the provinces would not be so infrequent and a few years later some would also challenge the Budapest teams for the top positions, although none would triumph.

A developed rivalry between MTK and Ferencváros, which went down in history as the derby of the Örönkrangadó, the eternal rivalry. This rivalry involved various aspects, with sport just one. The FTC and MTK stadiums had been built one year apart, between 1911 and 1912, and a 20-minute walk from each other. MTK, whose stadium was built later, designed an improved version of the FTC stadium with a capacity of about 20,000 seats. To further strengthen their Hungarian identity, MTK had built their facility on a street called Hungária. Fans also claimed that while MTK played with the brain, Fradi played with the heart: probably a reflection of the social background of the two clubs.

Another obvious difference was in the selection of players; in the case of FTC, players were mainly from the ninth district, while MTK players came from other parts of the city. What they had in common were their origins: most of them, in fact, came from the lower-middle classes and many of them, more than half of the MTK players and a quarter of those in the FTC, were Jewish.

However, it is necessary to reiterate one concept: the distinction between Jewish and German-Christian clubs with reference to MTK and FTC was only really in the minds of the fans. MTK had from the beginning embraced a secular, liberal and open vision to athletes of any origin or religion and FTC admitted without restriction Jewish players among their ranks, unlike the Germanic associations and sports clubs of the past dedicated to other disciplines.

Between 1916 and 1925, MTK dominated football in Budapest, with FTC returning to the top only in the 1925/26 season, the year before Hungarian football became professional. And between 1926 and 1945 the most successful club was Ferencváros, despite the inclusion on the local football scene of a third contender, the Liliak – the nickname derived from the white and purple colours – of Újpest.

Over the years, moreover, a similar trend to Austria had developed: some players had begun to enjoy star status, including Imre Schlosser, who between the early 20th century and 1928 played for FTC and MTK and became top scorer of the championship seven times; Alfréd Schaffer, the MTK striker who at the end of his career crossed the path of a very young Matthias Sindelar to Austria Vienna; and in the years to follow Gyula Zsengeller and Gyorgy Sarosi, who were finalists at the 1938 World Cup.

The healthy sporting rivalry between MTK and FTC was for the first time undermined by the political difficulties that hit Hungary: at the end of the Great War, after the political gap between 1918 and 1919 that had seen the Socialist Republic of Bela Kun – born Abel Kohn – in power, Hungary lived through what American historians called 'White Hungarian Terror', a bloody and violent two-year period where communists and Jews had been the main targets of the politics and national propaganda supported by former Admiral Miklos Horthy, who came to power in 1919.

During these years, rivalry in the stadiums became heated and anti-Semitic epithets became more and more frequent. In addition, during the 1920s, '30s and '40s, many Jewish players left Hungary and landed in neighbouring countries. This was the case, among others, for Bela Guttmann, who had competed for Hungary at the 1924 Olympic Games and found refuge in Austria. Others instead abandoned the continent, such as Gyorgy Orth and Ferenc Sas – born Ferenc Sohn – who headed for South America. The process of Aryanisation led in 1939 to the commissioning of MTK – then called Hungária – and a year later to its dissolution.

During this period, Ferencváros became the team of a regime that after some initial resistance had decided to collaborate with the Nazis in the deportation of the Jews. And in 1944, Andor Jaross, Minister of the Interior and active in identifying and sending Jews to extermination camps, was appointed president of the club. Fradi was for the Hungarian regime what Schalke 04, in the early '40s, would have represented for the Third Reich: the team of the regime, an association that would increase the popularity of both sides. This association would have been facilitated by the fact that, although not all Fradi fans were supporters of the Horthy regime, many of them came from the ninth district.

The intensification of relations between Horthy and Hitler, moreover, had led many Fradi fans, mostly craftsmen, small traders and skilled workers, to come even closer to the ideas shared by the German and Hungarian governments.

The parable of Fradi must not, however, make us forget the past of the club, born as a team under whose flag the vast majority of proletariat members and citizens living in the suburbs had gathered. They were the only team that until the advent of Újpest had managed to compete with MTK in terms of results and fan numbers. In many of the suburbs where there was no top-line team to take part in the championship, the choice between MTK and Ferencváros was usually easy.

Over the years, far-right fans had also begun to identify with other clubs such as Csepel, Gamma and UTE. These were located in the Aryanised industrial centres of the country and would especially in the case of Csepel, undoubtedly the strongest of the three, have obtained exclusive benefits during the war such as the possibility to preserve their athletes from military service or in other cases to see them leave the capital only for short periods of time. For many, the successes of Csepel in 1941 and 1942 were helped by such favours.

## 3

AMONG THE independent states that had formed following the dissolution of the *Vielvölkerreich* – the empire of many nations and ethnic groups – of the Habsburg monarchy, there was also Czechoslovakia, which, like the other nations belonging to the empire, retained a rich and fragmented multi-ethnic identity. It was populated by numerous Jewish communities, active in sports as well as in the liberal professions and commercial activities that had given rise to secular or Zionist multi-sports. Another of the ethnic groups present in the newborn Czechoslovak Republic was the Germanic one, settled mainly in western and northern Bohemia and which in 1930 represented 25 per cent of the population. The latter was also active in sport, mainly in disciplines such as football and winter sports.

Prague, moreover, had given birth to the Sokol, which could be translated into a hawk, a gymnastic movement of enormous importance that would later be exported to other regions of the empire, thanks to the Bohemian immigration of those years.

In the aftermath of the First World War, the newly formed Czechoslovakia had established itself as one of the leading nations in European sport and would remain so until 1945, when the communist regime reorganised the sport, using it as a propaganda vehicle. Before the outbreak of the Second World

War, the Holocaust and the ensuing ethnic cleansing, different nationalities and ethnic groups had more or less peacefully coexisted within the region: the term *Konfliktgemeinschaft*, coined by historians and which translates into 'conflict communities', well reflected the Czechoslovakia of the time. In this context, sport had taken on the role of a glue between the different cultures that populated the region.

The advent of football took place at this very stage. From 1896 the first amateur championship was born, which would continue until 1925, the year of the turning point towards professional football. From the very beginning, the teams of the capital were the masters: between 1896 and 1902, the title was raised exclusively by teams from Prague. The first of these was CFK Kickers Praha, followed by Deutscher FC Prag, one of the many clubs born within the German community that populated the city. DFC Prag in those years were considered one of the strongest teams in the empire, so much so that between 1897 and 1899 they would remain unbeaten for about two years. But already the rivalry that would later characterise Czech football, between Slavia Prague and Sparta Prague, had taken hold.

Throughout the inter-war period, crowds flocked to the stadiums in Prague, reaching peaks of 50,000 for national team matches and when Czechoslovakian club teams challenged Austrian, Hungarian or Italian teams, as was the case, for example, in the Mitropa Cup matches. Even in Czechoslovakia, the greatest players of the time became celebrities. Karel Pešek-Kád'a, Josef Bican and Raymond Braine would be part of a 'Golden Age', as it was called. The era that began with the end of the Great War and the birth of the First Republic saw Sparta Prague and Slavia Prague share almost all of the national titles until 1938. Both would also win the Mitropa Cup, Sparta twice and Slavia once. The greatness of the Czechoslovak football movement was also evidenced by the national team's achievement at the 1934 World Cup, when they reached the final against Italy. Over the years, although the communist regime would dissolve or rename several of the capital's historic clubs, the national team would still achieve some success, such as a second place in the 1962 World Cup and a European Championship title in 1976.

However, it would be impossible to tell the story of Czechoslovakian football without delving into the history of the two teams that characterised it most of all. In Prague, even more than in Vienna and Budapest, it had been a two-horse race since the very first years. The period between 1897 and 1902 saw the undisputed domination of Slavia Prague, who won the championship six times in a row. And in the following years, until 1918, the local titles remained in the capital, divided between Starometský SK Olympia, Sparta Prague – winner of their first championship in 1912 – and Deutscher FC Prag. In 1918 the Slavia–Sparta duopoly began, which has survived almost intact until the present day, except for a few sporadic intrusions by some other teams. The transition to professional football had not changed the situation: until 1939 the rivalry would remain a private affair between the two main teams of the capital with one exception, the victory of Viktoria Zizkov in the 1927/28 season, the team from a suburb that had been annexed to the capital for five years.

Slavia Prague was founded in 1892, a year earlier than Sparta. The origins of the two companies were similar; both were founded by young entrepreneurs motivated by the desire to create a sports club. In the case of Slavia, they were medical students who wanted to spread the practice of sport to their colleagues. Slavia was born in the form of a multi-sports club, and after cycling in 1896 it had included football among its disciplines. It was in that very year that the first derby against Sparta took place. Slavia Prague owes to John Madden, Scottish footballer and coach, probably as much as MTK in Budapest and Austrian football owes to Jimmy Hogan: Madden exported to Prague an innovative style that coincided with the beginning of an era that lasted for about 25 years. Since the founding of the Mitropa Cup, Slavia were a permanent presence and reached the final in 1929, losing to the Hungarians of Újpest but raised the cup in 1938 thanks to the achievements of Josef Bican. During the war years, the championship continued and Slavia put on the board four more successes and two second places, in both cases behind Sparta.

Sparta Prague was founded in late 1893 by a group of boys led by three brothers: Václav, Bohumir and Rudolf Rudl. Initially, the Athletic Club Sparta Praha – the club's first name – wore its famous tricolour uniform, where red stood for the symbol of the royal city and blue for Europe, but yellow is still a mystery today. A few years later, however, the Sparta players began to wear a black-and-white-striped tunic with a big 'S' that stood out on the front. But in 1906, following a trip to London, then-president Petřík decided to replace the striped shirt with a red uniform. The reason? Petřík had seen an Arsenal match and fell in love with the Gunners' strip. From that moment on, Sparta would keep red as its main colour alongside the white of its socks and shorts.

Once the Great War ended, before which the city's most decorated club had been Slavia Prague, the era known first in Czechoslovakia and later in the Czech Republic as 'Sparta d'Acciaio', which would continue during the 1920s and 1930s, began. In fact, with the exception of the period between the 1919/20 and 1924/25 seasons, Slavia and Sparta shared all the titles until the 1938/39 season, when the championship was suspended due to the outbreak of the Second World War. Fans were able to admire their first favourites such as Peyer, Hojer, Perner, Káďa, Kolenatý, Červený and a few years later Hochman, Burgr, Hajný, Šíma, Silný, Čtyřoký, Košťálek and, above all, Oldřich Nejedlý, the top scorer at the 1934 World Cup in Italy. Before the beginning of this glorious phase, Vlasta Burian, who would become the king of Czechoslovakian comedians a few years later, was among the stars of Sparta. The club's two winning periods also included victories in the Mitropa Cup in 1927 and 1935 (a third final was won in 1964, but at that time the importance of the competition had greatly diminished).

Even before the Austro-Hungarian Empire was dissolved, newspapers and magazines entirely dedicated to football were available and would be published until 1945. In addition, radio became an important means of communication in sport: the Prague journalist Josef Laufer was one of the pioneers of sports news at European level and in 1926 he would be one of the first to report a football match on the radio.

During the First Republic, football had also become a literary subject: two of the leading Czechoslovakian writers of the time, Eduard Bass and Karel Poláček, penned successful stories about the world of football that would later be repackaged in a cinematic key. For example, *Klapzubova jedenáctka*, the *Klapzuba Eleven*, was a fairytale written by Bass, steeped in satirical and political elements about a football team made up of 11 brothers trained by their father, a Czech farmer. In 1930 Karel Poláček wrote *Muži v offsidu Ze zivota klubových páivrženců* (*Men in the Outcast: On the Life of Team Fans*), the first book published about the most popular sports fans in the world.

Sparta and Slavia also represented an invaluable resource for the national team, which at its height had reached the 1934

World Cup Final thanks to champions such as goalkeeper František Plánička, nicknamed the 'Bohemian Swallow', a legend of Slavia Prague, Czechoslovakia's Antonín Puč, and Oldřich Nejedlý. Josef 'Pepi' Bican, who became a legend of Czechoslovakian football after a previous life in Austria, also won the Mitropa Cup with Slavia and was the tournament's top scorer ten times.

There were those who had moved to Czechoslovakia for economic and professional reasons, such as Raymond Braine, who became the first Belgian professional footballer. In 1930 Belgian football was still amateur and in order to convince players not to flee abroad, the clubs gave them unofficial salaries paid under the table. But in many cases this income was not sufficient, and some players had set up commercial activities. One of the most common practices was the opening of cafeterias. As the years went by, this trend became more and more frequent, so much so that the Belgian Football Association published a communiqué that read as follows, 'Since it is considered essential to block the phenomenon of players as cafeteria owners, the Executive Committee decides that, except for those players whose parents have owned a cafeteria for more than five years, permission to open a cafeteria will be granted only and exclusively on the condition that the player is not part of the team.'

Braine had been one of those players who had opened a cafeteria, and came to his decision to emigrate abroad. First he moved to England, where he was unable to obtain a work permit, and then to Prague, with Sparta. In 1935, when Sparta won the Mitropa Cup, Braine scored three goals in the two legs of the final, cementing his legendary status.

# II

# HUGO MEISL: THE FATHER OF MODERN FOOTBALL

*'Here's the Schmieransky team, happy?!' Hugo Meisl, who arrived by taxi at Café Ring, a downtown club he regularly frequented, after having put his hat on the coat rack, slammed a sheet of paper on one of the tables in the café, causing surprise among the journalists present. That paper reported the 11 who would take the field against Scotland a few days later. Schmieransky, a term that only a Viennese citizen could invent or understand, was a word composed of two parts: Schmieren, whose meaning is 'to write without knowing anything', and -ky, a suffix typical of the surnames of Czech and Polish immigrants, usually first-generation Viennese who barely spoke German. In other words, Hugo Meisl had self-deprecatingly called himself ignorant and illiterate and had prepared the team by giving in for the first time to the insistence of journalists. There was a name that had been repackaged in previous months in Viennese sports newspapers to which the coach had always given little credit: Sindelar. Meisl had finally decided to give the champion*

*of FK Austria a chance to lead the Wunderteam attack, and not just any game. This time Sindelar wouldn't have lined up on the right side, but in the position that was most familiar to him: centre-forward. The perception that the press had of Sindelar clashed with that of Meisl: for the press, Sindelar was the undisputed star of Austrian football; for Meisl, instead, he was one of the many players at his disposal. Following that friendly match at home against Scotland on 16 May 1931, the Austrian national team would become the Wunderteam for everyone.*

1

ON THE football field as well as on the battlefield, as a coach or as secretary general of the ÖFB, the Austrian Football Association, Hugo Meisl was been awarded honours in whatever role he held. His brother, sports journalist and former goalkeeper Willy Meisl, called him 'the Pitt, Disraeli, Bismarck and Napoleon of Austrian football' in one. He had become a leader on the Isonzo during the Great War years and would become one a few years later at the helm of his creation, the Wunderteam. The team was imbued with the innovative and revolutionary spirit of its coach and shaped according to the Scottish concept of the passing game, developed according to the characteristics of its interpreters. Those of technique, talent and boldness that Viennese players had cultivated since childhood on the outskirts of the capital.

Between the two football schools of the time – the English and Scottish – Meisl never had any doubts: he had chosen the Scottish approach, which preferred quick passes and interchanges between players to the hardness and rigidity expressed by the English. His life, interrupted at the threshold of the Second World War, had seen him fight at the front and distinguish himself in the world of football as a player, referee, coach, secretary general of the ÖFB and co-director of the magazine *Sport-Tagblatt*, as well as having covered in his youth a series of jobs that had led him to live and work abroad, between Trieste and Paris. The story of Hugo Meisl is partly forgotten, despite his position as an essential component in the development of football as we know it today.

Hugo Meisl was born on 16 November 1881 in Maleschau – today's Malešov – in the then Kingdom of Bohemia, at that time a province of the Austro-Hungarian Empire. The mother tongue of the Meisl family, however, was German: the Jewish community of which little Hugo's parents were part came from the small mining town of Kutna Hora, at the time known as Kuttenberg, where 40 per cent of the population spoke German. However, Hugo grew up bilingual because Czech was spoken in the region. The family moved to the Austrian capital in the last decade of the 19th century, where Hugo also decided to dedicate himself to football because other sports, such as gymnastics, were forbidden to Jews at the time. In 1895, when he was only 14 years old, he joined Vienna Cricket and Football Club. He served three years for the club and participated in the qualifying match for the first edition of the Challenge Cup against Wiener AC along with only two other Austrian players, since at the time all the remaining members of the team were English.

However, his career as a player did not produce the results he had hoped for and Meisl decided to take up refereeing. It was at this stage that young Hugo began to develop the skills that would make him an absolute authority in Austrian football first and then in the international game. At the same time, in order to carry on his passion, Meisl had rolled up his sleeves. The income was small – football was still amateur – and to undertake a paid profession that would allow him to maintain himself and support his large family was necessary, since, in the year of his arrival in Vienna, 1895, Willy, the sixth child of the family, was born.

In 1897 the Meisl family moved to the second district of the capital, Franzenbruckenstrasse. After finishing his studies without a diploma, Hugo found his first job in a local company, Jg. Simon, but only two years later he decided to leave Vienna for Trieste. His father had pushed for this in the hope that his son would undertake a commercial career at the expense of a sporting one. Hugo worked for two companies and then returned to the Austrian capital in 1902. Hugo, however, both in football and in life in general, showed an incredible curiosity and was always attracted by the possibility of new experiences. In fact, he stayed for only one year in Vienna and left again for Paris. Here he was hired by the company S.Chartet, but the French experience soon came to a close. Meisl had become fluent in French, Italian and English, as during his stay in Trieste he had undertaken a trip to England in order to perfect the language. Over the years he would also try his hand at studying Spanish, Dutch and Swedish, thus mastering seven languages in addition to German. This knowledge would be extremely useful to him at the end of the war, not only in the role of coach but also that of journalist, since he would write for various local and international newspapers. In particular, he would become a columnist for the *Neue Wiener Sportblatt*, a newspaper that closed in 1921 due to high production costs.

However, the dream of making his way in the world of football had not waned; far from it. Having maintained various contacts within Austrian football, Meisl was perfectly aware of how the sport had evolved. One was Johann Leute, one of the most popular Austrian players of the time, who kept him up to date with developments. When he returned home, Meisl also resumed playing for a short time. He was nicknamed *Hirnfussballer*, the player with the brain, because of his intelligence, which was much more important to his game than physicality. However, the playing interlude was short, and Meisl returned to refereeing with for more encouraging results: in just one year he was hired by ÖFV as secretary responsible for refereeing matters, which was a complicated role at the time as the public often ignored the rules of the game. To address this he also wrote a dedicated manual. In 1904, when he was only 23 years old, he became the first secretary general of the ÖFV, founded on 18 March by the two oldest clubs in the capital: First Vienna and Vienna Cricket and Football Club.

Outside the world of football, Meisl was contracted by the Länderbank, the country's first bank, while his career as a referee and manager of the ÖFV went on smoothly: in 1907 he officiated his first international match – a friendly between Austria and Hungary – and was among those who represented Austria at the FIFA congress in Amsterdam. Only a year later he became secretary of Vienna Cricketer and Football Club, which changed its name first to Wiener Cricket in 1910 and later, in 1911, to Wiener Amateur Sportverein, today's Austria Vienna. He held the position of manager, also carrying on his commitments with the ÖFV and those of coach of the national team, because with the upcoming Olympic Games – which at the time represented the only international stage for football – Meisl wanted to create a competitive national team.

In May 1912, after a disappointing 1-1 draw against Hungary which would soon be followed by other unsatisfactory results, Meisl asked the referee of that match, James Howcroft, if he could recommend a coach he could trust to lead the national team at the Olympic Games in Stockholm. He was directed to James 'Jimmy' Hogan, an English compatriot coach of Howcroft's who at just 28 years of age was already sitting on the bench of the Dutch Dordrecht team. Like Meisl,

Hogan had not been very successful as a player either. He had brief spells as a forward at Burnley and Bolton Wanderers, and as a coach he was immediately inspired by the principles of the passing game, developing a cohesive style focused on ball possession.

The first team to show off this style of play was Queen's Park, founded in Glasgow in 1867. That approach – in addition to the original definition of a passing game – was recognised by many as 'combination football', and utilised dribbling in very rare cases. Such a style required greater organisation and synergy between players and departments. It was not by chance that one of the first English teams to adopt it was Royal Engineers AFC, composed of military personnel. It was football using short passes and quick exchanges, through which the teams always tried to keep the ball on the ground.

Hogan accepted the assignment, and after a spell as coach of the Amateure – taking over from Meisl, who in the meantime had changed roles – he took charge of the Austrian national team. He immediately insisted on training based on the use of the ball, partially to the detriment of heavy physical and athletic sessions. The approach that Hogan and Meisl were about to develop would take precedence over any other aspect. Hogan, who during his first days in Vienna had described the amount of meat consumed by Austrian players as 'frightening', was one of the first to introduce personalised diets.

Before Hogan's arrival, the difference between English and Danubian football had been obvious. On some occasions when English teams had played in Vienna against the newly formed continental teams, the visitors had scored double figures. And at the national team level, the outcome was the same: in a 1908 tour, England beat Austria 6-1 and 11-1, Hungary 7-0 and the Kingdom of Bohemia 4-0. In the following years, thanks to several British coaches who left their homeland to seek their fortune in continental Europe, the gap between the English and continental games began to shrink. Hogan was the architect of the first success of an Austrian team against an English one, when Amateure defeated Sunderland 2-1. Hogan was convinced that the English were obsessed with physical condition and that they ignored ball control, as evidenced by the weekly sessions of some of the English teams around the early 1900s that only used the ball twice a week.

Hogan and Meisl agreed on a 2-3-5 formation, which was particularly in vogue at the time. This scheme, also called the pyramid, would remain a constant over the years. It was an idea which might seem inapplicable nowadays – based on the assumption that the two defenders, called full-backs, would take care of the opponent's forwards, that the lateral midfielders would take care of the opponent's wingers and at the same time they would widen during the possession of the ball while the midfielder ideally had two qualities: vision, having to act as playmaker, and the physicality that would help him to recover possession. The second key figure was that of the *centre-forward*, who, contrary to the modern conception of the role before being a scorer, had to be able to back up and put his team-mates, the inside-forwards, in goalscoring positions. Then there were the wingers, usually freed from defensive tasks. Another system was 3-2-2-3, which included a stopper at the expense of the central midfielder.

Thus was born one of the most prolific partnerships in football history, and years later Hogan would say of Meisl, 'The greatest man I've ever met in the world of football … I have great respect for Herbert Chapman, but I've never met a football man like Meisl. He knew the style of play and technique of any nation.'

The relationship that had been established between the two was also highlighted by a curious anecdote. In later years, Hogan, whenever he would accept an assignment with a foreign federation or team, would always have a clause included in his contract that would have freed him in case of a call from the ÖFV.

After some initial communication problems often solved by Meisl's intervention, Hogan had earned the trust of the players he had selected for the 1912 Olympic Games in Stockholm. Austria's results, however, were not exciting, as the team was eliminated in the second round by Holland and would lose the consolation final against Hungary.

Meisl later demanded Hogan's assistance for the 1916 Olympic Games, which did not take place because of the war, and also in preparation for the friendly against England in 1932, then for the 1936 Olympic Games in Berlin, where Austria showed up with an amateur formation and were defeated in the final against Italy after a fortuitous goal scored by Annibale Frossi. In the 1934 World Cup, the collaboration between the two had not been possible: Hogan's fees were too high owing to the disastrous finances of the Austrian federation.

In 1914, the outbreak of the First World War interrupted their ambitious project. At the British Consulate in Vienna, Hogan was told that the risk of armed conflict was far away, and that he could continue to carry out his duties without problems. But two days later, war was declared. Meisl would be summoned to the front, and Hogan ran into even more serious problems: he was arrested as an 'enemy on foreign soil'. Fortunately he was saved by the intervention of Alfred Brüll, president of MTK in Budapest, who put him under contract as a coach in 1916.

Meisl spoke both German and Czech. This made him free from the communication problems occurring among the ranks of the various divisions of the Austro-Hungarian army. When he arrived in Ljubljana, the temporary headquarters of his regiment, he was assigned to Battalion 29 of the Landsturm. On 1 November 1914 he was appointed lieutenant in the empire's campaign against Serbia. Not much is known about his experience at the front, but it is known that he fought on the Isonzo and took part in the 11th battle, the one in which Matthias Sindelar's father died. Some of the honours he was awarded are also known: in 1915, in Krn, on the Soča, he was awarded the *Signum Laudis* – the Military Medal of Merit awarded in Austria between 1890 and 1918 – then a Silver Cross of Merit the following year, a Third Class Cross of Merit in 1917 and the *Verwundetenmedaille* – Medal of the Wounded – on 29 January 1918, after having saved several battle companions during an avalanche. With the end of the Great War and the foundation of the First Republic of Austria, Meisl resumed his work from where he had left off.

## 2

IN THE context of the crisis of the years following the end of the First World War, Hugo Meisl was fortunate: he was able to resume his work commitments at the Länderbank and also his sports commitments, dividing his time between administrative matters, the role of national team coach, referee and manager at Wiener Amateur SV. He also had two further appointments: columnist for the sports magazine *Sport-Tagblatt* and entrepreneur, as in February 1920 he had founded Stadion, a company producing sporting goods. He moved to Fasanengasse, a street in the third district of Vienna, then in 1919 he married Maria Bican and after the birth of their eldest daughter the family moved to Krieglergasse, also within the third district of the capital.

One of Meisl's battles was the establishment of a professional championship in Austria. An advantage of switching from amateur to professional football was the possibility for clubs to earn more money and for players to receive legal salaries. After all, football had by now become a mass phenomenon and a media and social product in the wake of the English game.

It had become the sport of the proletariat and the working classes, and match attendances had increased accordingly. But not everyone agreed: for many the burdens that this model implied would be problematic.

Nevertheless, Meisl continued in his battle and on 21 September 1924 he succeeded: the Austrian championship became professional. As the coach claimed in an interview in 1926, the introduction of professional football was 'actually a practice to reimburse players for expenses incurred, a practice that already existed during the war years'. According to the coach, the only difference was that payments were now made in a legal and justified form.

There is no doubt that Meisl's initiative was also observed with interest in some neighbouring countries. In Czechoslovakia, football became professional in the 1925/26 season and such a development followed in Hungary only a year later. Despite this, some side-effects did not take long to appear such as the exorbitant demands from the main stars – called *Kanonen* – of salaries that their clubs were often unable to sustain. To mitigate the problem, sponsors often intervened. In addition to wages, however, clubs had to face a number of other charges that were not even covered before, such as maintenance of the playing fields and advertising expenses.

Just as he had fought to make football professional, Meisl put just as much effort into making it an international phenomenon, both for club teams and national teams. The goal was always the same: to ensure that clubs and federations could earn money by exploiting the enthusiasm of the public on a local and global scale. Thus, in 1927 Meisl conceived the Mitropa Cup, for central European teams. In June 1927 a congress was held in Venice at which delegations from Austria, Hungary, Czechoslovakia, Italy – although the Italian teams would begin to take part in the competition in 1929 – and Yugoslavia were present. At first, however, the tournament was not recognised by FIFA, and was competed for in a private agreement between the federations. When Austrian football became professional in 1924, Deutscher Fußball-Bund (DFB)

– the German football federation – proposed the exclusion
of Austria from FIFA because ÖFB had ceased to abide by
the rules of amateur football. Furthermore, the DFB did not
intend to compete with professional teams, either at club or
international level.

Meisl's impetus for the restructuring of European football
came from a challenge between First Vienna and Sparta
Prague at the Hohe Warte Stadium, which attracted only
3,000 spectators. Thus a competition was born in which, as
Meisl said, 'the best central European teams would have the
opportunity to participate and win a valuable trophy'. The
proceeds would allow the clubs to avoid the exhausting foreign
tours that for some time before had been a major source of
income along with some sporadic friendly matches that Meisl
organised against English teams.

In the same way and in the same year as the Mitropa
Cup was founded, the Švehla Cup – known in Italy as the
International Cup – was also created. It ran until 1960,
although the 1936–38 event was interrupted because of the
Anschluss, the annexation of Austria to Nazi Germany. One
of the objectives of this competition was the re-establishment
of diplomatic relations between nations that had fought at the
front. Hugo Meisl had hated his experience at the front and
this had motivated him to bring the nations together through
his greatest passion, football. This tournament, which did not
have a fixed duration even though each edition lasted about
two years and worked in the format of a championship –
with home and away matches and a final league table – was
competed for by Austria, Italy, Hungary, Czechoslovakia,
Switzerland and in the last edition also Yugoslavia.

The event for professionals was flanked by an amateur
edition, which was held on two occasions between 1929 and
1934 and in which Poland and Romania, rivals of national

amateur teams from Hungary, Austria and Czechoslovakia, were each playing once. Thanks to their presence in the International Cup, the Austrian national team were back in international competition. Their last appearance was at the 1912 Olympic Games, as in 1924 and 1928 the Austrian federation had been excluded because it had already turned to the professional model.

Hugo Meisl was not the only one to fight for football to distance itself from the amateur model: in France, among those who showed the same vision was Jules Rimet. The president of FIFA since 1929, Rimet shared the idea that football should become professional by separating itself from the model promoted by his compatriot Pierre Le Coubertin, inventor of the Olympic Games. Rimet's mission was to make football 'a means of understanding and friendship among the youth of the world', in an attempt to open up the sport to the people and to allow young people raised in modest environments to earn a living through their performance on the pitch. Compared to Meisl, Rimet denounced the elitist nature of football and sport in general: amateurism, according to him, represented a means of confining sport to certain privileged castes.

## 3

AN IDEA of how Meisl intended to shape the Austrian national team is shown by an interview with *Mundo Deportivo*: 'When a club in the capital has in its hands a [talented] young man of 15 or 16 years they communicate it to me, and from that moment I start to keep an eye on him by putting me in direct contact with him, and thanks to my advice and teachings I start to train him as a future international player. This system has the advantage that players start to respect me right away and my authority is absolute. What's more, in doing so, I have the utmost confidence in them. This is the basis for my stay in the difficult role of coach. I am a true friend to the players: with them I share joys and sorrows and I would share, if necessary, even the worst injustices. But always on the condition that maximum discipline reigns among them.'

Meisl was one of those coaches who didn't stick to any single training methods, and if necessary he had no problem experimenting with new solutions despite going against the opinions of the fans and the press. Sindelar, for example, was one of those players who did not immediately enjoy the unconditional trust of his coach. Meisl often preferred other strikers to him, such as Karl Jiszda or Franz Weselik, and later on also Friedrich Gschweidl, who although not a great goalscorer possessed other qualities such as an impressive physique and an excellent heading ability. Over time, however, thanks to the emergence of Sindelar at Austria Vienna and the absence of some Rapid Vienna strikers due to commitments in the Mitropa Cup, Meisl began to use Gschweidl and Sindelar at the same time in the hope that the two, thanks to their different characteristics, could work together. Sindelar, however, being more versatile, had to adapt and often had to move to the right.

In some cases, however, despite some good performances with the national team and with Austria Vienna, Meisl had to change his approach. On 6 January 1929, after a 5-0 defeat against a German regional selection made up mainly of players from FC Nürnberg and Greuther Fürth, he had quarrelled with the player and decided to exclude him for several matches. This was due to a post-match discussion when Sindelar claimed that the team should play with shorter passes despite the ground being soaked with water. Meisl did not agree at all and a disagreement broke out.

The press ran an unconfirmed quote from Meisl, 'Never Sindelar again!' However, in 1930, after Meisl had returned to Vienna after a period of illness, Sindelar regained his place, showing that perhaps the tension between them had faded quickly. Despite few goals being scored, Meisl continued to alternate Sindelar with Gschweidl. On a personal level, there was mutual respect between Meisl and Sindelar: Sindelar saw in Meisl an absolute authority and Meisl saw in Sindelar a football genius. More generally, Meisl always tried to keep a distance between himself and his players, which is why he called Sindelar 'lei' and Meisl addressed Sindelar as Mr Sindelar.

But the relationship between the two had never blossomed. On the one hand, Sindelar represented for Meisl the ideal player to play the role of centre-forward, that in Meisl's mind meant the player had to drop deep and provide assists for his team-mates. On the other hand the friction between the two had repeatedly caused Meisl to leave out the Austria Vienna man. Moreover, Sindelar regularly complaining about his knee had represented a further problem. Meisl was repeatedly tempted to replace him with Josef Bican, a young forward with whom the coach had immediately impressed because of his hunger for goal, technique and speed.

Sindelar's performances in the Austria Vienna jersey, not least the successes in the Mitropa Cup, convinced Meisl otherwise. At the end of the 1934 World Cup, however, the time seemed to be ripe: Sindelar was almost 32 and Bican was at the start of his career. Only the latter's willingness to move to Czechoslovakia prevented Meisl from carrying out his plans.

# 4

HUGO MEISL took charge of 122 matches when he led the Austrian national team from 1919. Of those, 66 were won, 29 were drawn and 27 were lost. Many great players were picked and lots of praise was handed out by the local and international press. There is no doubt, however, that the golden age of the Wunderteam coincided with the Sindelar era, when the star of Austria Vienna found a regular place in the side.

Between 1931 and 1936, Austria established themselves as the best team on the continent. On 16 May 1931 they beat Scotland 5-0 in a friendly match. With their usual aplomb, the UK newspapers had taken their hats off to that performance. In the *Athletic News*, journalist Ivan Sharpe wrote, 'In the 1920s and 1921, English and Scottish football had reached their peak. In that period, England triumphed against Scotland 5-1 at Wembley and in the return match Scotland won 5-1 at Glasgow. The two teams that won these matches played very well, but I think that the current Austrian national team is better than both.'

It was on that very occasion that Meisl's team was renamed 'Das Wunderteam', the Wonder Team. There were those who, like Josef Gerö, president of the Vienna Football Association, claimed that this was the most important success of the Austrian team at international level and those who, like Sindelar, at the end of the match underlined the evident technical gap between the two teams, with Scotland unable to display the style of play that had made them famous in the world.

Within a few months, Austria inflicted two humiliating defeats on Germany: 6-0 at Berlin on 24 May and 5-0 on 14 September, in Vienna, in front of 50,000 spectators. German coach Otto Nerz's approach of making 11 changes to his line-up for the second match was worthless and Sindelar, now a fixture in the team, scored a hat-trick.

Other overwhelming victories were those against Switzerland and Hungary. Meisl's men won 8-1 in Basel and 8-2 against Hungary in front of 60,000 spectators in Vienna.

On 28 October 1932, following Czechoslovakia's victory over Italy, Austria won the second edition of the International Cup and were then invited to play in London against the English team, an honour until then granted only to Belgium and Spain, in 1923 and 1931 respectively. The precedents were not encouraging: in 1923 England had defeated Belgium 6-1 and in 1931 they had beaten Spain 7-1. Austria didn't head to Stamford Bridge in good form: the Wunderteam had produced some unconvincing performances against some minor Viennese teams. An article published in the days leading up to the match claimed that instead of England v Austria, the public would be watching England v Rudy Hiden. Meisl himself, in an article written for the German press, had argued that this was not the best time to face the English.

Meisl recalled Hogan, who called the invitation to prepare the Austrian national team on that particular occasion 'the greatest honour of my football career, and a splendid gift for my 50th birthday'. In fact, Hogan's presence had been made possible by the intervention of another great coach of the time:

Herbert Chapman. Chapman, with his enormous influence in the world of football, had managed to convince Racing Club de Paris – a team with which Hogan had signed a contract – to release the coach during the two weeks preceding the London match. It was Chapman who had organised the Austrian tour so that the team could stay at the Hotel Oddenino and train at Arsenal's facilities. Meisl was as close to Chapman as he was to Hogan, although Chapman and Meisl's interpretation of tactics differed considerably. If Meisl had espoused the Scottish style, Chapman based his approach on restarts and counter-attacks. But on a personal level the two were extremely close to each other, as evidenced by the fact that Meisl named one of his sons Herbert. The friendly in London was a chance for Meisl and Hogan to show the English founding fathers the progress of continental football.

The duo imposed strict rules that prevented players from having any contact with their families from 10 to 28 November and opted for an unusual preparation compared to the one usually adopted. As the Spanish magazine *Blanco y Negro* wrote, Meisl organised three weekly conferences on the history of British football, and only once a week they trained with the ball. The sessions would mainly focus on the use of the upper body and knowledge of the British style of play.

The referee appointed was the Belgian John Langenus, the most respected official of the time at international level. On 1 December, the Austrian team left for London from Westbanhof station. They were greeted by thousands of supporters and a climate of total enthusiasm. The players smiled and hardly anyone refused to take pictures with the fans. The days before the match were marked by comments from newspapers, such as the *Daily Mail*, which wrote, 'We must not forget that the Austrians have brilliant players. I know, for example, that Sindelar is worth exactly the same as the best English forwards: he is brilliant at controlling the ball and he finishes just as well with both feet. And both Zischek and Hiden are first-rate players.'

In Vienna, Heldenplatz was overflowing with spectators. Three huge loudspeakers had been positioned in order to listen to the commentary of Willi Schmieger and Balduin Naumann. The Parliamentary Committee on Finance had postponed its meeting.

There were about 42,000 spectators at Stamford Bridge, a very low number given the scale of the event, but it reflected the mood of the evening: England would have an easy game.

In fact, England scored in the first few minutes, confirming the feelings of the days before the match. Goalkeeper Hiden, perhaps under pressure to play under the eyes of Chapman, the coach who had insisted on him at Arsenal, had not been impeccable. The quality of the Austrians began to be noticed but the English scored again and in the 27th minute they were 2-0 up.

Only then did Austria start to up their game. Smistik and Sindelar took control but the most active player was Zischek thanks to his raids on the right. At the beginning of the second half, Hiden saved a Houghton shot and shortly afterwards, at the end of a combination between Sindelar, Schall and Zischek, the ball ended up in the English net for 2-1. Austria held England in their area with a series of corners and Nausch hit the post before Schall's effort was saved by the English goalkeeper, Harry Hibbs. England recomposed, and after two excellent parries by Hiden, they scored again with a free kick from Houghton.

But the 3-1 scoreline was misleading as the Austrians were proving superior at times, and then Matthias Sindelar took over. After receiving the ball from Vogl, he moved forward, avoided a couple of tackles and made it 3-2. The goal was applauded by the English public, who had begun to get excited about the Austrians long beforehand. Referee Langenus said after the match, 'Sindelar's goal was a masterpiece that nobody else could do against the English. Nobody before or after him.' It was a goal comparable to that scored by Diego Maradona in the World Cup against England 54 years later. But in the 82nd minute, a long-range finish by Sammy Crooks surprised Hiden and put England 4-2 ahead. Five minutes from the end, Zischek scored again after a corner kick, and later on England had a goal disallowed as the match ended 4-3 to the home side.

English forward Billy Walker said that if they played a second match, the English would score eight goals. However, press opinions tended to agree that if Austria were able to capitalise on all the opportunities they created, the game would certainly end differently.

Years later, Willy Meisl recounted an anecdote that clearly showed the impression that the Wunderteam had left in England, 'A few years later, when I moved to England, I went back to Stamford Bridge. I knew a note had been reserved in my name. I shyly asked, "Do you have an envelope for Meisl?" The person in charge started flipping through the huge stack of letters while I began to think that he didn't understand my pronunciation or that the note had never been reserved. So, I started spelling my name while the person in charge found the envelope. He handed it to me with the firmness of a sergeant, which he had probably done in the past, and quietly and honestly said to me, "I will never forget this name as long as I live."'

The press not only gave detailed reports of the match, but also focused on some individual performances. Anton Schall was described as a 'first-class strategist', but the display of Matthias Sindelar was particularly praised. A journalist from the *Daily Herald* wrote, 'Sindelar is the best centre-forward continental Europe has ever known. I don't remember a play, a touch or a feint of him made not for the benefit of his own team.'

# 5

MEISL AND his parents had a complicated year in 1933. The national team's performance was unstable, which was a big problem, since a year later they would compete in their first World Cup. It was clear to everyone – especially the press – that Meisl's men were no longer as brilliant as they had been only one or two years previously. 'Once upon a time there was Wunderteam,' wrote *Sport-Tagblatt* after Austria's 2-1 home defeat against Czechoslovakia. One of the players in the coach's sights was again Matthias Sindelar. In an interview, Meisl declared, 'I feel compelled to inject new red blood cells into the blood of our old, anaemic Wunderteam. Time passes for everyone, and Sindelar is obviously no exception. The repeated and exhausting meetings with his club over the past few months have prompted me to make that decision.'

However, these beliefs were shaken following Austria's 5-2 friendly defeat of Hungary, only about 40 days before the start of the World Cup. On that occasion Sindelar was almost unanimously the best player on the field, and *ABC* wrote that he was 'completely obscuring Sarosi'. Zischek, Bican (2), Viertl and Schall scored, with Sindelar as the main creator, so Meisl decided to retrace his steps and bet on the Sindelar–Bican pairing for the World Cup.

The Italian experience, marked by swinging performances and often heated disagreements, had left a lot of bitterness in the ranks of the Austrian national team. But there wasn't even the time to shift disappointment of the defeat as Meisl and his team had to return to the final phase of the International Cup, with the hope of defending the title won two years earlier as partial consolation for a World Cup gone wrong. The results, however, were not the best and it was Pozzo and Meazza's Italy who won that edition.

The criticism focused mainly on Matthias Sindelar. After the 3-1 International Cup defeat against Hungary, the newspapers – probably for the first time – expressed their scepticism about the physical condition of the player, saying they were in favour of rejuvenating the formation. The *Wiener Sonn-und Montags-Zeitung* wrote, 'It seems obvious that Sindelar needs rest. Lately he lacks dynamism, he plays softly and slowly and unresolved.' Even those who had at first criticised Meisl for the choice to exclude Sindelar on some occasions began to take the coach's side. Hugo Meisl's authority was not affected both locally and internationally, as demonstrated by the fact that at this stage Meisl boosted the career of a very promising young coach named Bela Guttmann, a former acquaintance of Viennese football having won a national title with Hakoah Vienna, earning him a contract with the Dutch club of Sportclub Enschede.

The swansong for Meisl was the victory in the friendly played on 6 May 1936 against England. The coach decided that he would bet on the old guard, not wanting to take the risk of deploying a too inexperienced side and consequently throwing away the opportunity for a rematch against the English. Meisl was not so much afraid of the quality of the English team, which was in his opinion at the same or lower level than the Austrians, but the speed: precisely for this reason he offered cash prizes for those who would win races over 60m, 100m, 200m and 400m.

The English, just as two years previously, were mostly represented by Arsenal players, although Chapman had left the Gunners' bench two years beforehand. The exceptional circumstances had made ÖFB think about every detail, which is why, as in the London match four years earlier, Belgian referee Langenus had been chosen. For the occasion, Austria wore a red uniform with white borders. After only 20 minutes the 60,000 spectators were already in raptures as Austria were ahead by two goals thanks Viertl and Geiter. Sindelar, with two assists, seemed irrepressible and had repaid with interest the trust his coach had placed in him. The match ended 2-1, and Camsell's goal in the 54th minute did not change the outcome. It was the first time that Austria gave the impression that the supremacy of the English over continental football had begun to falter, and all this thanks to a coach who many Austrians had begun to doubt.

ON A human level, few people didn't love Hugo Meisl. Karl Heinz Schwind, director of the *Kronen Zeitung* newspaper for several years, after meeting some of the protagonists of the Wunderteam, wrote, 'Meisl was loved by everyone. Today, however, the players often complain about training.' Josef Smistik once said, 'He was our God.' His decisions were accepted by everyone and no one ever dared challenge his authority. One example was Peter Platzer, a world-renowned goalkeeper who had had to accept Rudy Hiden's reserve role for years.

Once, during a training session in Budapest, there was a funny episode: Meisl started chasing Wudi Müller with a hat in one hand and a stick in the other. The player, guilty of venturing into a risky dribble that ended with the loss of the ball, had sent his coach into a rage. Müller said he had never run as fast as he did that time in an attempt not to get caught.

Meisl died on 17 February 1937 at the age of 55 from a heart attack, a problem that had already manifested itself years earlier when the coach had left Vienna for a short period of time to seek treatment. Meisl was in the offices of the ÖFB, intent on questioning Richard Fischer, a young First Vienna prospect, about his age. Fischer claimed to be 17 but Meisl was not convinced: he remembered an interview with the coach of First Vienna three years earlier in which he understood that Fischer was already 17 at the time. All of a sudden Meisl nodded to Fischer, sat down and a second later collapsed. Fischer didn't waste a second calling for help, and the ÖFB leadership hurried to call Emanuel Schwarz, doctor and president of Austria Vienna. But there was nothing to be done: Schwarz arrived on the scene and could only confirm the cause of death.

The first condolences came from the upper echelons of the ÖFB, an institution that owed a great deal to the work carried out over the years by Hugo Meisl. Richard Eberstaller, who was its president, wrote in a statement later taken up by *Sport-Tagblatt*, 'At the moment it is impossible for us to estimate the weight of this loss, but the merits of Meisl remain immense. Thus, I can only express my personal grief and mourning in all members of the Association, as it does in the entire football community. He has represented the essence of the enthusiasm that has been created for football, not only in us but all over the world. As the great professional he was, he was able to bring all his expertise to football.'

The funeral was held on 21 February. Among the guests were almost all the players trained by Meisl over the years. Some – like Josef Bican – also came from abroad. Amid tears and emotion, it was former captain Walter Nausch who said, 'I approach the coffin in the name of the team that Hugo Meisl created, representing all the active players. We are forever separated from our dear friend Hugo Meisl. We Austrian players will never forget him.'

Condolences also came from abroad. Jules Rimet, with whom Meisl had collaborated in the creation of the World Cup, arrived in Vienna for the funeral. Tributes for the coach of the Wunderteam also came from foreign newspapers. *The Excelsior* in Paris greeted Meisl as 'the Napoleon of Austrian football', while Italy's *Gazzetta dello Sport* wrote, 'There is no

Italian sportsman who was not deeply moved by this loss. Italy has lost a friend and a battle companion who has worked hard with all his energy to promote the interests of Italian football.' The Hungarian newspaper *Nemzeti Sport*, on the other hand, recalled its commitment at international level and its battles to promote cooperation between nations.

Inside the museum of Austria Vienna, an entire 20m² hall has been dedicated to the memory of Hugo Meisl where some of the objects that decorated his office in Karl-Marx-Hof are on display: an armchair, a coffee table with two chairs, cushions, a shelf and a desk.

# III

# THE BOHEMIAN IDENTITY OF THE WUNDERTEAM: IMMIGRATION IN THE HABSBURG ERA

*You often hear stories about football stars who grew up in poor conditions and became champions. In addition to talent, the common thread that links these stories is a hunger to obtain through sport a redemption and a social recognition otherwise unthinkable. Austria, one of those countries that emerged battered from the Great War, would have represented a fertile ground for two entire generations of football aces. From the rubble of the first post-war period, the Wunderteam had blossomed, and from the defeat suffered in the Second World War a team capable of imposing itself at international level would have grown. Many of these boys came from the outskirts of Vienna: Favoriten, Ottakring, Rudolfsheim and others. And many of them were children of economic migrants from Bohemia and Moravia, some of the poorest regions of the empire. It should also be remembered that in 1924, and consequently in the period between the two wars, football in Austria had become professional and being a star meant not only gaining popularity but also money; much less than a player receives today but much more than a boy born and raised in one of the suburbs of Vienna earned at that time. Compared to other sports traditionally consumed by the aristocracy and the city's elite, football was open to everyone: a ball was enough to play it, even assembled with rags if necessary, and a game could take place almost anywhere; in an abandoned car park, in a garden or along a quiet street. Its democratic and transversal nature had made it the sport of the masses. And only a few years later the whole nation would reap the benefits.*

# 1

DURING THE Habsburg hegemony, waves of migratory flows had taken place from the countryside to the big cities. The most coveted destination was the capital of the empire, Vienna, where hundreds of thousands of migrants had settled not only from the Austrian countryside or less crowded cities, but also from other territories gathered under the crown such as Hungary, the Kingdom of Bohemia, the Margraviate of Moravia, and Silesia.

Most of these new resources were used in the brick or clothing industry. In the latter, Bohemian workers were often employed as tailors or shoemakers, and many of their children would study in dedicated institutions so as to give continuity to their parents' profession. Some statistics report that in 1910 the proportion of Bohemian students in clothing schools was close to 67 per cent. Women, on the other hand, were mainly employed as cooks or carers. Already by the second half of the 18th century, Bohemian immigration to Vienna had become widespread. In a first phase, the suburbs in which the migrants settled were mainly Landstrasse and Wieden, in the third and fourth districts of the capital respectively.

According to an informative report of 1778, in these areas the main language was not German, but Bohemian, which from the 19th century onwards was officially called Czech. It was in Bohemian that most public communications were issued for the residents of the area. Towards the middle of the 19th century, a second wave of migration took place from Bohemia and continued uninterrupted until the outbreak of the Great War. The new infrastructure and buildings on either side of the suburbs, together with the real estate boom in the city centre, required more manpower. The revolution in Vienna took place in 1848, and in 1857 Emperor Franz Joseph I of Austria decided to remove the city walls that hindered the development of a rapidly expanding city.

Many Czech and Moravian workers were then hired to redesign the Ringstrasse, removing the fortifications and walls and building a very long avenue flanked by majestic buildings. The evolution of Vienna as an international metropolis had become public knowledge across all regions of the empire and had led to the arrival of a large number of skilled and unskilled workers. Once again, much of this flow had come from Bohemia and Moravia.

In 1885, between the areas of Wienerberg and Laaerberg, two of the districts most populated by Bohemian immigrants, the Prater was built, initially conceived as a recreational area for the benefit of the working classes. Many of the so-called 'Ziegelböhmen', a derogatory term translated into 'Bohemian bricks' by which the Viennese citizens used to refer to the Bohemian bricklayers who came to the Austrian capital, were exploited by their employers. It was a condition to which the 'Maltaweiber', the mortar workers, were also subject. In some cases, the workers stayed crammed into common rooms and were paid in tin coins accepted only in taverns and shops that had agreements with the employers of the factories where the workers worked.

The Ziegelböhmen and the remaining families staying in the peripheral districts of the capital were documented in various publications of the time. The *Denskchrift der Vororte*

– *The Suburbs Memorandum* – wrote in 1884 about the situation in the Favoriten district, 'Here workers spend less, and traders and producers sell cheaper goods than in the city centre.' Favoriten was probably the district with the lowest rental costs, far below the prohibitive prices in the city centre.

According to the 1900 census, the main language of 102,974 Viennese inhabitants was Czech, and in Favoriten this proportion reached a peak of 25 per cent. Thus, Vienna had become the first Bohemian city after Prague. In addition, of Favoriten's 133,009 inhabitants, 23,437 were Bohemians.

In 1895, the anger of the workers resulted in a strike that forced industrialists to renegotiate working conditions with their employees. Some of the results of the protest were the granting of regular wages, an 11-hour working day – the days used to last 15 – and Sunday as a day off.

In the following years, several Bohemian cultural associations were founded, some of which survive to this day. Workers' associations had not been the only ones to proliferate in the capital. At the beginning of the 20th century, in fact, the Bohemian community had also created other associations such as the Slovansky Zpevacky Spolek, a music club founded in 1856, the cultural centre Slovanska Beseda, founded in 1865, and the Akademicky Spolek – Academic Association – founded in 1868. Although the Slovak population was a minority compared to the Bohemian one, this too gave rise to some associations: one of them, Tatran, enjoyed great popularity among Slovak students.

The first Czechoslovakian sports club was founded in 1866 under the name of Sokol, or falcon, a club dedicated to gymnastics. In 1910 Sokol included 15 clubs in and around Vienna – some of the most important were Sokol Vidensky, Sokol Fügner or Sokolska Jednota – and had about 2,800 members. In 1902, the Delnicka Telocvicna Jednota – the

Association of Social Democratic Workers – founded the
football club SK Slovan, which still exists today and at which
Antonín Panenka played many years later. In addition to
having built the Franz Horr Stadium – which for many years
would host the home matches of FK Austria – between 1922
and 1925 under the original name of České srdce Stadium, the
club would go down in history for having reached the final of
the Vienna Cup in the 1923/24 season, then lost in extra time
against Wiener Amateur Sportverein. SK Slovan – although
it was mainly known for its football team – was actually a
multi-sports club, also having a cycling team and an athletics
team. In 1935 it changed its name to AC Slavia and in 1940
to AC Sparta. Over the years, several other Bohemian football
clubs had sprung up in Vienna – such as SK Moravia, which
later merged with SK Cechie, SK Slavoj, Videnske Slavie or
Wienerberger – but none achieved the results and popularity
of SK Slovan. AC Sparta were one of the few Czechoslovakian
clubs not to be dissolved after the German invasion, but despite
this its survival was repeatedly questioned. The Aryanisation
policies implemented by the National Socialist leaders often
prevented players of Bohemian origin from taking part in the
games and forced club secretary Alois Janousek to resign from
his post. The battle to maintain their Bohemian identity was
also tough: the Germans wanted to rename the club Eintracht
or Germany X, and only the intervention of an ÖFB official
put paid to the invaders' intentions. But despite this the Nazis
never thought of banning the club because more than 50 per
cent of its athletes had meanwhile joined the Wehrmacht.

# 2

ONE OF the suburbs that needed more manpower was Floridsdorf, on which there was a large industrial area. Companies such as Siemens & Halske, Clayton-Shuttleworth and FIAT had their plants there. Among the companies that populated the Floridsdorf district, many worked in the textile and food industries.

Admira Wien, which over the years would become one of the capital's leading teams, was closely linked to the Hermann Pollack's Sohne company, dedicated to the processing of cotton fabrics from Bohemia. Equally important was Simmering, a district that hosted important local and international realities such as the Maschinen- und Waggonbau-Fabriks-AG or the Apollo-Kerzenfabrik, which had given work to many Bohemian, Hungarian, Bulgarian and Croatian workers.

One of the main activities to which the workers devoted themselves in their free time – one of the most important achievements after their uprising – was football, a particularly popular pastime among the children of the workers who benefited from the vast prairies closed to the circulation of vehicles, such as the area of Laaerberg, between Favoriten and Simmering. Simmeringer SC, in the district of Erdberg, was created by 20 children who, like many of their peers, used to kick the famous *Fetzenlaberl* [homemade footballs]. Their intentions were facilitated by the help of a former nurse from the abandoned Blatter hospital who donated the locker rooms once used by hospital staff to the local boys.

In 1937, a report revealed that about one-third of Austrian professional players came from the suburbs of Favoriten and Floridsdorf. It was no coincidence that a few years earlier, when Austria had visited Italy as one of the favourites for the 1934 World Cup, Hugo Meisl had proposed a line-up with seven players of Bohemian origin, including Karl Sesta – who was born as Karl Szestak – Franz Cisar, Josef Smistik, Karl Zischek, Johann Urbanek, Matthias Sindelar and Josef Bican, not to mention that Meisl himself was born in Bohemia.

From the very first years when football had spread to Austria, some of the players who were the children of the melting pot that characterised the Vienna of the Habsburgs had been attracting the attention of the general public. In some cases, their attitude on the pitch faithfully reflected the difficulties they suffered in their youth.

One such player was Karl Sesta – one of the many footballers of the time born and raised in the Simmering district – who after embarking on his career as a blacksmith had become one of the strongest defenders of the time. His career had actually begun as an attacker, but the physicality with which he faced his opponents meant that he was moved to the defence. He was nicknamed 'Der Blader', the fat man, and was distinguished by two things: his intolerance of authority, the main reason why, in 1938, he would not fit into the plans of the German coach Sepp Herberger; and his ability to forcefully put his opponents to the ground, ordering them to get up. Often and willingly, Sesta became the main target of the opposing fans who did not spare him whistles and insults.

But eclipsing even Sesta, the player who more than anyone else had reflected the anger and moods of the suburbs of the time was Josef 'Pepi' Uridil, nicknamed 'Der Tank', the tank.

Sesta and Uridil often left the field to the talent of boys who spent hours and hours in the gardens and flowerbeds and who would prove decisive in shaping the Austrian style of play during the following years. Before Matthias Sindelar there had been Johann Studnicka – and ten years later Josef Bican would appear.

# 3

JOHANN STUDNICKA was one of the leading players in the Austrian team for the Olympic Games in Stockholm in 1912. He played alongside the star of the then Amateure, Ludwig 'Luigi' Hussak, a figure we will examine in the following pages. During the event he scored two goals: one in the 5-1 first-round against Germany, and a second in the semi-final of the consolation tournament in which the previously eliminated teams took part, against Pozzo's Italy, a match that ended in favour of the Austrians.

In fact, the feat against Germany had been facilitated by the injury of the German goalkeeper Albert Weber. Replacing an injured player was only possible with the consent of the opponent. The Austrians had said no to the Germans' request, although it is still not clear whether that was by the choice of their captain or their ignorance of the rules. In any case, in the second half Studnicka and his team-mates scored the goals to confirm the win.

Before participating in the Olympics, Studnicka scored three times in the first international match played between two non-British national teams, in 1902, when Austria had inflicted a very heavy 5-0 defeat on their Hungarian cousins in Vienna. A year later the script would repeat itself: Austria beat Hungary 4-2 with Studnicka again scoring a hat-trick.

In those years, Wiener AC, where Studnicka played, was the most successful team in the capital and five or six of its players regularly appeared in the Austrian national side. Among them was also Alexander Popovich – nicknamed Xandi, or Poperl, also of Bohemian origin. In 1910 he stopped playing football to become one of the founders of Wiener Amateur SV, which until then had been, under the name of Vienna Cricket and Football Club, the most bitter rival of Wiener AC both in the league and in the Challenge Cup.

On a technical level, many in Vienna attributed to Studnicka the invention of dribbling, a game made effective by the small stature of the player. The cartoonists of the time enjoyed portraying his rounded legs and the supporters of Wiener AC claimed that the player commissioned his tailor to make deformed trousers in line with his physical structure. As well as Studnicka's successes with his national team, he also achieved honours with his club: he won the Challenge Cup three times, in 1901, 1902 and 1903, making Wiener AC the most successful team of the time in that competition.

On a local level, during those same years, Studnicka was just as successful in winning the first edition of the Tagblatt Cup – the Austrian championship held between 1900 and 1903. As a coach, he won a national title at the helm of Zurich, a team he had come to after two uninspiring years at First Vienna.

However, Studnicka's popularity was never comparable to the level Uridil and Sindelar would later reach: the reason was the low popularity of football at that time. In Studnicka's years, attendances at matches were not at all comparable to what could have been observed in the following years: if you look at some of the matches that Austria played over the years against Hungary, you can see that in 1919 Josef Uridil scored a goal in front of 20,000 spectators, a number that had tripled in 1932 when Sindelar had put in a masterful performance against the Hungarian team, culminating in an 8-2 result. Twenty years earlier, when Austria had lost the [consolation] final against Hungary at the Olympic Games in Stockholm and Studnicka was on the field, only 5,000 had been present.

# 4

JOSEF URIDIL, born on 24 December 1895 in Ottakring, a suburb of Vienna and the son of a Bohemian tailor, would become the first true favourite of the Viennese crowds. He had chosen the profession of footballer because, as he admitted, that job allowed him to dedicate himself to football every day from late afternoon. He was not the first talent from the suburbs to amaze his audience, but compared to his predecessors he was able to perform at a time when football had definitively established itself as the most popular sport in the country, the sport of the proletariat. There was talk of football in the suburbs as much as in the more affluent neighbourhoods, and the football stars began to appreciate the status that celebrities from other worlds enjoyed. From this point of view, Uridil was Sindelar's predecessor, although as we will later observe, the similarities between the two were few.

In his autobiography published in 1924, Uridil wrote, 'I developed a passion for football at an early age, and when I was ten I started kicking a ball. It was a pleasure for me, although it was also a pain in some cases because in every game we kicked the shit out of each other. But that never stopped me as Hasnerstrasser from challenging the Brocken – well-dressed and stylish men – of Koppstrasse the next day.'

A few years earlier, when he was in his early 20s, he had written on the 20th anniversary of the founding of his club, Rapid, 'I'm 23 years old, and I'm confident that my 81 kilograms can sustain the white and green colours for at least another eight years. I wish everyone the same success in football that I have had. Despite the fact that my mother still waits for me on the doorstep with rolling pin and other blunt objects from time to time, our club's motto remains the same, "Hurrah for the green-white colours, the champions of Vienna."'

During the years following the end of the Great War, Vienna was packed with champions and nothing suggested that Uridil would impose himself on everyone else and become a true folk hero. The legend of Uridil began in 1922, when the famous singer-songwriter Hermann Leopoldi wrote the song 'Heute Spielt der Uridil' ('Today plays Uridil'). Football and music – two of the most popular folk cultures in Vienna at the time – had come together.

The song, a lively ballad, became one of the most popular in the 1920s. A photograph from 1923 portrayed a band of Rapid fans welcoming the team on the field and singing the song dedicated to their leading player in the derby against the city rivals of the Wiener Amateur Sportverein. This song also gained popularity among those who did not share the same passion for football, thus contributing to its fame. Shortly afterwards, Uridil would also appear on the big screen: in the film *Pflicht und Ehre* (*Duty and Honour*), Uridil played himself and in the same year, 1924, the writer Alfred Deutsch-German – a fictional name – published a novel of the same name.

His popularity rose even outside the Rapid fans thanks to his feats with the national team, despite the fact that he was only able to take part in friendly matches throughout his career. At the first possible opportunity, on 5 October 1919 – the first match of the Austrian national team since the end of the Great War – Meisl summoned a then 24-year-old Uridil who repaid him by scoring in front of 20,000 spectators: Austria beat Hungary 2-0 and the Meisl cycle began again after the interruption after the First World War. With Rapid, as well as in the national team, Uridil had found his ideal partner in Richard 'Rigo' Kuthan, three times top scorer in the Austrian championship between 1913 and 1922.

His technical feats were acclaimed everywhere and his name began to appear on boxes of chocolates, bottles of fruit juices, spirits, soaps, wines and sportswear. A famous sculptor presented his bust at an important exhibition and many other artists wanted to paint him.

Uridil had started his career with some minor clubs and then moved on to Rapid before the outbreak of the First World War. There is no doubt that Uridil was the first true representative of the 'Rapid spirit'. His finishing ability is corroborated by the statistics of the time, according to which the goals he scored throughout his career would have totalled around 1,000. Here is a testimony of the time:

'There had been scorers before him, but none of them possessed his incredible impetus and the irresistible force he displayed on the pitch. Those who dared get in the way of that race car were wiped out. They were run over, almost destroyed and decomposed in their chemical constituents. Rivals trembled when the small but robust Uridil launched one of his devastating attacks. Usually, such actions ended with Uridil and three or four opponents on the ground, and the ball in the net.'

This was the Der Tank (an Italian army tank), a great player capable of making his team win matches by scoring prodigious goals. One of his most classic moves was as the lone striker starting from his own half, which most of the time ended with the ball in the opposition's net.

In spite of everything, Uridil proved capable of staying grounded. He was regarded by all as an honest citizen and a man of the people who in time had even grown tired of his own fame. In an interview he declared, 'People allow themselves to do what they want with me, but the only thing they can't do is to say that I am a bad footballer.' He played practically his entire career at Rapid – except for a small interlude at First Vienna – and ended his career in 1928 before coaching several clubs around Europe.

Reluctantly, he joined the Wehrmacht during the Second World War and returned to Rapid in 1954, this time as a coach and won a championship. Unlike Sindelar, his fame faded almost completely over time, except in the Viennese suburbs. However, it is important to point out that Uridil and Sindelar were only alike in terms of popularity. Friedrich Torberg, a writer and frequent visitor to Vienna's coffee houses, once said, 'Uridil and Sindelar, in reality, can only be compared in terms of popularity: on the level of technique, creativity and skill there was the difference between a tank and a wafer.'

# 5

JOSEF BICAN had been was one of the many talents who blossomed in the fringe of Vienna and would begin to take his first steps in the world of football around the age of nine. His father, František, was born in a small South Bohemian Region town called Sedlice u Blatné, had been a footballer and had played for ASV Hertha Vienna. In 1922, when he was only 30 years old, he died from an injury in a match against SK Rapid. Money was scarce, and František could not afford much for his family. Josef Bican remembered his humble origins several times: he claimed that the fact that he had had to play barefoot for years and could not afford football boots helped him to forge his technique.

Josef grew up perfectly bilingual in Czech and German. His parents had enrolled him and his two brothers at the Janos Komensky school – the same school Matthias Sindelar had attended a few years earlier – in the district of Favoriten.

Coincidentially, his uncle happened to be a friend of Matthias Sindelar: the two lived on the same street, Quellenstrasse, and grew up in the same neighbourhood.

At the age of 15, Bican was hired by Farben-Lutz and was thus able to play for the company team, Schustek-Farben. Here he was noticed by Roman Schramseis, an SK Rapid defender who had been a Schustek-Farben player in the past and hadn't lost the habit of going to see his old team play when he could. Schramseis offered him the chance to join SK Rapid and Bican, after an initial reluctance, agreed. Club president Dyonis Schönecker gave his approval so that the player could become an integral part of the SK Rapid youth line-up.

Legend has it that after only one training session and one match with the youth team, Bican was promoted to the SK Rapid amateur team and was guaranteed a salary of 100 shillings per month. After three months he switched to the professional team and scored 52 goals in 49 games in four seasons, despite the fact that he felt that the Rapid style was not for him: he considered himself a refined player and as such he would have hoped for a transfer to Austria Vienna, where Sindelar's star shone. The two, by the way, faced each other for the first time in the very year in which Bican had become a professional player. SK Rapid won 5-3, and Bican scored twice.

For a few years, Bican would have had as his attacking partner Matthias Kaburek, another boy of Bohemian origin who grew up in the suburbs of Vienna, and who one year before Bican's arrival at SK Rapid had raised the Mitropa Cup by scoring a goal in the final against Sparta Prague.

Over time, however, Bican became increasingly undisciplined, suggesting that his dissatisfaction at of SK Rapid had increased. An offer came from Slavia Prague, but a move did not materialise due to resistance from SK Rapid. A little further on, however, came a second approach, from Admira Vienna: his uncle – who, if necessary, acted as a agent – had for some time established relations with the society of Jedlesee, at the time the strongest team of the capital. Bican decided to move, despite the fact that SK Rapid had offered him a substantial increase – which was a rare deviation from the club's policies – and that the player would not be able to play any matches for the rest of the season, as his contract with SK Rapid remained binding.

During his time at Admira Vienna – the team with which he won his second championship and scored 18 goals in two seasons – Bican was sought again by Slavia Prague, who offered him 600 shillings a month, an impressive figure if you consider that the average salary of a worker of the time amounted to 18 shillings.

So Bican decided to change clubs again, although the problem was always the same: how to solve the contract's sticking points? This time the suspension from playing would have lasted for four years, but thanks to a Slavia lawyer who personally went to Vienna the situation was resolved. Slavia paid a substantial sum to Admira and managed to regain the player's passport, which had been confiscated in the meantime. Bican returned to his beloved Sedlice u Blatné, his father's hometown and where he went every year as a child to spend the summer with his grandparents.

At Slavia, Bican would continue the memorable career he had embarked on in Austria. He won the Mitropa Cup in 1938, the year after his arrival in Prague, along with six national titles and he finished as top scorer in the championship ten times. His Czechoslovakian career was divided between Slavia Prague, Sokol Vikovicke Zelezarny – a second division team now called FC Vitkovice – Spartak Hradec Kralove and back to Slavia, which meanwhile had changed its name to DSO Dynamo Praha at the behest of Komunistická Strana Československa, the Czechoslovak Communist Party.

Having changed nationality, however, Bican was unable to take part in the 1938 World Cup as the bureaucratic process for obtaining a Czechoslovakian passport took longer than expected and ended about a month after the conclusion of the tournament. Bican made his debut with his new national team on 7 August 1938, scoring three goals. A year later he faced Nazi Germany in a friendly, having refused an invitation to represent the Germans only a year earlier, defending the colours of the newborn Protectorate of Bohemia and Moravia. The match ended 4-4 and Bican scored a hat-trick.

At the end of the Second World War, Bican received several offers from Italy, but he never took them into consideration: he hated the Nazis as much as he hated the communists, and was convinced that the Communist Party would come to power in Italy. Unfortunately, it was Czechoslovakia itself that would end up under Soviet influence a few years later. Bican, whose dislike for the communists was notorious, became a sworn enemy of the regime. His wife would tell of how the couple were spied on relentlessly, but thanks to the footballer's notoriety and fame their protection would still be guaranteed.

At the end of his career, Bican also coached several Czechoslovakian teams including Slavia, and he died of a heart attack in December 2001 in a hospital in Prague. Four years earlier the IFFHS – the International Federation of Football History & Statistics – had awarded him the title of Best World Cup Scorer of the Century, in conjunction with Uwe Seeler and Pelé. When asked why fewer talents were born compared to his golden years, Bican had answered, 'Because so many talents were born ... well, there was no food after the war, we children were poor. Back then I never saw kids around on mopeds.'

## 6

THE IMPACT of Bohemian players on the Austrian team's results continued in the years following the war, although the Wunderteam era was in the past. The only link with the pre-war period was Walter Nausch, who had captained the Wunderteam and would be the national side's coach during the 1954 World Cup. Austria came third, improving on Meisl's fourth place 20 years earlier. Despite the fact that in 1954 the team's reputation as a footballing power had faded, there were those who placed Nausch's men among the favourites behind the defending champions Uruguay and the *Aranycsapat*, the Hungarian team that, like the Austrians, had experienced a second youth at the end of the Second World War.

Nausch decided to rely on two Bohemian players. One was goalkeeper Walter Zeman, who earned the nickname 'The Panther' after a sumptuous performance against Scotland on 13 December 1950. However, in the eyes of his coach, Zeman would have been the reserve for First Vienna's Kurt Schmied. Zeman lined up in the semi-final against Germany after Schmied suffered a heart attack in the quarter-final against Switzerland. But Zeman's performance – at the time he starred for SK Rapid, where he won eight national titles, an Austrian Cup and the only edition of the Zentropa Cup in 1951 – didn't live up to his nickname and proved Nausch's initial choice correct. He conceded six goals and was responsible for the first two.

And then there was Ernst 'Stoissi' Stojaspal, one of Austria's greatest post-war scorers, who was famous for his ability to perform tight dribbling in spite of his slight build and exclusive use of his left foot. Of Stojaspal, Emanuel Schwarz, his president at Austria Vienna, once said, 'We have a player who shoots with one foot, but he is still our best scorer.' With Austria Vienna, Stojaspal won three national titles, two cups and was the top scorer of the championship five times. Stojaspal ended his career in France and after hanging up his boots he opened the Café de Vienne in Monte Carlo, a coffee house in pure Viennese style which, as his wife Yvonne declared in an interview, he struggled to manage as his French had not improved over the years.

Ernst Ocwirk – born Ernst Ocvirk – was not of Czech descent but his story is not too different from that of his team-mates. Alois, his father, was of Yugoslavian origin but like Zeman and Stojaspal he too grew up in Ziegelböhmen circles. Ocwirk, nicknamed 'Ossi', grew up in the Floridsdorf district and soon became a fervent supporter of Admira Wien, the team that dominated Austrian football at the time.

In his book *Weltbummel: Vom Ballschani zum Kapitän des Kontinent-Teams*, the player said that he immediately fell in love with the Jedleseers' kit. But Ocwirk never had the chance to wear Admira's black-and-white-striped jersey: at the Stadlau, where the player started his career, he was noticed by the ex-Wunderteam midfielder Josef Smistik who transformed him into a midfielder – he used to play in a more advanced position – and tried to take him to his old club, SK Rapid, but Austria Vienna proved to be smarter and put the young talent under contract.

In 1971, when Admira merged with SC Wacker Wien, Ocwirk had the opportunity to coach the team he supported as a child. At the national level, he had been at the heart of the Austrian squad that had taken part in the Swiss World Cup. The journalist Norbert Adam painted a portrait of him in his book *Österreichs Sportidole*:

'His elegant style of play, his precise 40-metre passes, his correctness made him an example; he was an athlete and at the same time a gentleman. He was a simple man capable of giving nobility to the game of football.'

In an interview given to *Ballesterer* magazine at the end of 2013 at the Gerhard Hanappi Stadium, Alfred Körner and Theodor Wagner, two of the survivors of the 1954 World Cup, answered questions about their former captain. One was why Ocwirk's leadership was undisputed and why, of all the stars who played for the Austrian national team in those years, it was Ocwirk who was elected captain. Wagner's response was particularly interesting, 'He knew how to stay in the field like few others. There was never a time to take him back. The times he felt like he was playing badly, it was the end. He was always hypercritical of himself and always questioning himself. Although he was always trying to achieve important successes, he was the first to point out his mistakes. He was a perfectionist. Once, after he had become Admira's coach, I went to a training session: both on a technical and tactical level, he was a spade above all others.'

During the Second World War, Ocwirk, like many other boys whose origins were not in Austria, was relatively fortunate: although the Nazis were openly anti-Slavic, many of the children of immigrants of foreign origin retained their original nationality because they had not obtained an Austrian passport during the years before the conflict. For this reason they were stateless and as such could not be summoned to the front. After leaving Austria Vienna in 1956, Ocwirk joined Sampdoria, becoming the first Austrian player in the history of the Italian club, and at the end of his career he also coached them. In 1982, Vienna named a street, Ocwirkgasse, after him.

# IV

# THE FOUR VIENNESE SISTERS: FOUR FACES OF THE SAME CITY

*Between 1924 and 1938, years that marked the transition to professional football and the return to amateur football, the Austrian – or Viennese – football scene was the richest in central Europe. It saw four teams dominate and win the championship in turn. There was First Vienna, Baron Rothschild's team, SK Rapid, which immediately assumed a proletarian identity; FK Austria, which better than any other club represented the bourgeois spirit of the city centre; and Admira, another team born and raised in the Viennese suburbs. Five teams won the Austrian championship during its first professional phase, but one of them, Hakoah Vienna, one of the partly forgotten football stories of those years, had soon faded. Hakoah was part of a Zionist club that admitted only Jewish footballers among its ranks and that had been born with a very precise social purpose: to defeat the false anti-Semitic myth of the Jew being unfit for sport. In the years before 1924, the club had made its way to fourth place in the 1920/21 season, the year after its promotion to the first division, and second place the following season. But success came in 1924/25: in the previous years the team, already regarded as one of the capital's leading operator, had benefited from the arrival of important players from nearby Hungary. These included goalkeeper Alexander Fabian – who scored the decisive goal for the title after exchanging positions with an injured team-mate – Sandor Nemes, Josef Eisenhoffer, Erno Schwarz and, above all, Bela Guttmann, who years later would become one of the most successful coaches in football history. When Hakoah Vienna played away, anti-Semitic epithets were the order of the day. For many fans, facing the Hakoah meant facing 'the Jews'. However, from the summer after winning the league, Hakoah fell from title contention: many of its players had never returned from a tour to raise funds to finance the activities of the sports club. Their fame had made the major US clubs, the New York Giants and the Brooklyn Wanderers, interested in them and they offered contracts that the players could only dream of in Austria. From that moment on, the competition for the Austrian title would be down to four teams.*

FIRST VIENNA 1894, as its name suggests, is the oldest club in the capital. It was founded on 22 August 1894, and on the same day William Beale, one of its co-founders, designed its logo, which depicted three legs framing a balloon. The corporate colours, blue and yellow, were reminiscent of Baron Rothschild, the club's godfather.

Together with some cricket players, other men employed by Baron Rothschild began to play ball in the gardens near which they served. James Black, one of the Baron's gardeners, explained the rules of the game to the first members of the team. He and Franz Joli, the son of another of the gardeners, organised the first match: four Austrians against four Englishmen on one of Baron Nathaniel Mayer Anselm Rothschild's lawns.

Following that match and the consequent condition of the land, the Baron prohibited the practice of football on his property but proposed to finance the club. He paid the rent for a field suitable for matches, the Kuglerwiese, and was responsible for the costs of sports equipment. First Vienna was officially born.

The club in Döbling, the district where the Baron's residence was located, presented its articles of association a few days before First Vienna Cricket and Football Club, which is why it won the contest and on 22 August 1894 the club was officially founded. The request of Vienna Cricket and Football Club would be accepted just one day later, which is why the club had to give up 'First' in its corporate name. This was the beginning of a dispute that would take on not only sporting connotations over the decades.

The first clash between the two teams took place on 15 November of the same year at the Kuglerwiese, and Vienna Cricket and Football Club, which unlike First Vienna only selected English players, triumphed 4-0. Two weeks later, the return match was played at the Cricketers' ground, which ended with the same result. A year later, however, First Vienna won the derby – again it was 4-0.

In the very first years after the arrival of football in Austria, First Vienna became one of the leading teams of the city: in the first edition of the Challenge Cup they lost 3-2 in the semi-finals against the Cricketers. The following tournament was more favourable as First Vienna overcame the Cricketers in the semi-finals and in the final they demolished Victoria 4-1. It was the first title in the club's history and the second would come the following year: the 1899/1900 Challenge Cup saw First Vienna beat FC 98 3-1 and the Cricketers in the final, 2-0.

It should be borne in mind, however, that although the competition was open to all clubs playing under the Habsburg monarchy, in the first three editions only teams from Vienna took part.

Between 1900 and 1903 another competition was also held in Austria, the Tagblatt Pokal – Tagblatt Cup – the first competition to present the format of a championship. This one, compared to the Challenge Cup, admitted only teams from the Austrian capital. While the Challenge Cup can be considered a forerunner of the Mitropa Cup – and later the UEFA Champions League – the Tagblatt Pokal was the predecessor to the Austrian championship. However, the competition would only continue for four years as many teams left the federation. Moreover, due to the darkness coming in late during matches, they were often suspended and the remaining time was played several days later.

In those years, the teams gathered under the Habsburg crown also played each other in friendlies. Particularly noteworthy was the victory against DFC Prague in a match organised to mark the opening of the new First Vienna sports ground. DFC Prague, undefeated for two years, went to Vienna claiming that they did not want to win with a score higher than 4-0, so as not to spoil the party for the hosts. In response, the Yellow & Blue won 2-0 thanks to goals by Eipel and Gindl, two of the main players of the victories in the Challenge Cup. In the city, this result was also celebrated by the Cricketers. Towards the end of that year and the beginning of the following year, First Vienna, now composed exclusively of Viennese players, got the better of Slavia Prague, Graz, Wiener FC 1898 and Wiener AC.

First Vienna came sixth in the inaugural Austrian championship, and the following season they were eighth, but in 1913/14 they dropped to last place. Among other things, the club's managers were the protagonists of a resounding own goal: they had fought for the abolition of the play-off, which could have been a lifeline that season. So instead, First Vienna went down into the lower division.

The Döblingers decided to establish a parallel championship, the FUAN (Football Union of Austrian Nations), which lasted for only two years. Curiously enough, one of the teams that had joined the FUAN was SC Nicholson, who would rival First Vienna even later in the year. FC Nicholson had been founded by Mark Nicholson, the first president of ÖFU who was none other than the former First

Vienna player who only a few years earlier had played in the Challenge Cup Final.

In 1916, First Vienna were readmitted to the ÖFV and in 1918/19 they made their return to the top division. The year before the championship became professional, First Vienna came second behind Wiener Amateur SV.

The Döblingers were now an established part of the Austrian football scene, and the following year they finished third. It was no coincidence that Hugo Meisl began to call in a few First Vienna players more frequently to the ranks of the Wunderteam, such as defender Josef Blum, midfielders Gustav Chrenka and Karl Kurz and strikers Rudolf Seidl and Fritz Gschweidl. The latter would be Matthias Sindelar's main rival for a starting position as centre-forward for some years.

The first success for the club since the championship had become professional came in 1929, with a victory in the Austrian Cup against Rapid, followed by a second victory the following year. The first championship success came at the end of the 1930/31 season, with a 4-1 victory against FK Austria. Due to this triumph, the club qualified for the Mitropa Cup.

The team's development was confirmed in what was the greatest club competition of its time as First Vienna won the first and last Mitropa Cup in their history after beating Bocksai FC Debrecen, Roma and Wiener AC. The fact that the final had been played between two Austrian sides – and that the outgoing champion was another from the country, SK Rapid – gave a dimension of the importance that Viennese football had achieved in those years. Although Wiener AC did not win the league in those years, they included present and future members of the Wunderteam such as Hiden, Sesta and Cisar, who played that final as an attacker and was only a few years later back in defence during the World Cup. The following year the club came close to European success once again, but instead Schiavio, Sansone and Fedullo's Bologna won the title. The cycle continued, and confirmed the work done in the years before First Vienna won a second national title in the 1932/33 season. The following years were dominated by another club in the capital, Admira, but First Vienna still won an Austrian Cup in 1936/37.

Until 1938, First Vienna had had a large Jewish representation in their management ranks. The first president was Georg Fuchs, who was to be replaced by wine merchant Herman Schönaug. Until the advent of National Socialism, only two non-Jewish presidents had succeeded one another at the head of the club. But from March 1938, things changed dramatically. Moreover, in 1940 the club was forced to adopt the de-Anglicised name of Fussballklub Vienna.

The real golden age for First Vienna coincided with the inter-war period, when Austria had become Ostmark and the winner of the Gauliga Ostmark, as the Austrian championship had been renamed, would take part in the German championship and the German Cup, two knockout competitions.

Between 1942 and 1944, First Vienna won the championship three times in a row. In 1942 they could have reached the final of the German championship but were defeated 2-0 by Schalke 04, thus failing to emulate the feat of SK Rapid of the previous year. However, in 1943 came the success in the German Cup, thanks to a 3-2 victory against LSV Hamburg.

One of the key figures of First Vienna's success was undoubtedly Fritz Gschweidl: after winning two national titles and three Austrian Cups as a player, Gschweidl would win three more championships and a German Cup as a coach. First Vienna's success during the war years was partly due to the influence of its leaders in the army, which allowed the club to keep several of its players in the vicinity of the city and in positions that kept them safe from fighting or injury.

The story of Curt Reinisch, personnel director of the Military Health Administration of First Vienna, is interesting. Through his position, Reinisch was able to ensure that the First Vienna players could be classified as stenographers, nurses or medical staff assistants, thus being able to stay in the vicinity of Vienna. Reinisch, however, also acted as a guarantor for other teams such as Austria Vienna, who in previous years had been one of the most harassed clubs by the National Socialist regime. Reinisch was often in a position to guarantee players who stayed in hospitals longer than expected a longer period of leave without this encroaching on their presence on the pitch. He was investigated in 1944 and then released for lack of evidence.

On one occasion, Reinisch received an anonymous letter reading, 'It is easy to identify, especially in the case of First Vienna, players who attempt to ignore their duties as soldiers for the Motherland … Rumours of this injustice and deception have circulated in Vienna. For many years, we have witnessed citizens involved in the Great War – parents and parents' parents called back to the front while such healthy boys now remain in the suburbs – who now goes to fight? Coach Fritz Gschweidl himself was never summoned.'

Anyway, Reinisch managed to cover it up. The years following the end of the Second World War would see other clubs dominate the Austrian championship, especially SK and Austria Vienna. First Vienna would return to the top in the 1954/55 season, immediately after the World Cup in Germany.

# 2

SPORTKLUB RAPID – better known as SK Rapid – was
founded in 1897 in the Viennese district of Schmelz, about
one kilometre from where today's Allianz Stadium stands.
The club's mission from the very beginning was to 'involve
working-class sports enthusiasts in the game of football'. In
fact, only a few years after its foundation, the club had started
to play its home matches on Hütteldorfstrasse, which is why
the players and supporters were nicknamed Hütteldorfers.

The club was born under the name Erster Wiener Arbeiter
Fußball-Club, the first Viennese working-class football club,
but was forced to change its name only two years after its
foundation to Sportklub Rapid because of the concern the
club had begun to arouse among the authorities, given its
popularity among the working classes, who in the meantime
were also beginning to be represented politically. Despite this,
the proletarian and working-class connotation would continue
to accompany the green-and-white club for decades to come.

In the surrounding areas, as early as the end of the 19th
century, an urban and proletarian culture was already being
formed: many of the residents adopted SK Rapid as their
team. Not far from the SK Rapid camp, the first Viennese
workers' cooperative and orchestra was born, one of those
pastimes that were initially reserved only for the aristocracy
and the wealthier classes. Amateur sport also flourished on

the outskirts of the city, mainly fed by football matches. Soon afterwards, SK Rapid players would become local heroes. Most of them were children of families of economic migrants who came to the then capital of the Habsburg Empire in search of a better life, and who would find a vehicle for social redemption through football.

The main regions from which most SK Rapid players came were the Kingdom of Bohemia and the Margraviate of Moravia. Many of these families had taken up residence in the district of Schmelz, such as the Schedivy family, from whom the future members of SK Rapid Josef, Karl and Alois Schedivy, were born, and the Uridil family, who gave birth to Josef Uridil. The same origins were also shared by several managers, such as Karl Kochmann and Johann Holub.

Around 1900, immigrants from Bohemia and Moravia also began to populate other suburbs, including Ottakring, Rudolfsheim and Fünfhaus. The migratory flows that had helped to populate the suburbs did not of course only benefit SK Rapid: teams of immigrants, Videnska Slavie 14 among them, were born.

The hard life of the suburbs, in addition to the personal history that united the players, led to the creation of a strong feeling of team and unity. That spirit is still called *Rapidgeist*, a mixture of passion, attachment to one's origins and membership of the club. One had to feel proud to be a Hütteldorfer.

Hans Krankl, a prolific Rapid striker in the 1970s and 1980s, once said, 'A real Rapid player must be able to absorb the spirit of the club.' And in 1927, an article published in the *Illustriertes Sportblatt* said about Rapid, 'Throughout their history, they have hardly disappointed their supporters. They never give up until the final whistle. Rapid has its roots in the local suburbs and has never denied its territory.'

Behind the scenes, the key character was Dyonis Schönecker, the one who would be called the father of the *Rapidgeist* and the mind of the club. Not everyone loved him, however: for Schönecker, in fact, there were no distinctions between players. This meant that the most talented athletes did not have an easy time claiming salaries in line with their fame, even when football would become professional. At the heart of it all was membership of the club: being a Hütteldorfer was a faith, as evidenced by the way SK Rapid fans today still refer to their Allianz Stadium, which many call 'Sankt Hanappi'.

From the early years to the present day, the club has retained its traditional green-and-white kit, although the colour scheme has changed over time: during the 1920s, green stripes alternated horizontally with white stripes, while in the 1930s the shirt changed radically when a dark green uniform was designed with a horizontal white stripe in the middle. In the post-war period, the green-and-white stripes alternated again, although horizontally, in a kit similar to today's one.

In 1910 the club, which had been plagued by serious financial problems in previous years, took a decisive turn. Dyonis Schönecker, who had been an SK Rapid player since 1906, became the manager. At that time, in addition to the purely economic difficulties, the club had fallen into oblivion: the first land, located in Rudolfsheim, had been abandoned and several players and managers had packed their bags and let the boat sink.

The young Schönecker, assisted by one of the most influential players of the club at the time, Josef Schedivy, decided to start again from the basics, focusing on the SK Rapid youth team that in the meantime was showcasing promising youngsters like Josef 'Seppi' Brandstetter and

Richard 'Rigo' Kuthan, whose sister Emilie would marry Schönecker.

That team played in a very different way from the style that had initially characterised SK Rapid: ball on the ground and fast exchanges, with young players who seemed to be immediately adept in *Rapidgeist*.

It was thanks to Schönecker's work that SK Rapid once again dominated Viennese football over the next decade or so. In 1911 they won their first championship, thanks mainly to a trio of lethal strikers consisting of Gustav Blaha, Leopold Grundwald and Heinrich Körner. The first two would be summoned by Jimmy Hogan for the Olympic Games the following year.

Between 1911 and 1913, SK Rapid were the most successful club in the country with eight titles won. Not surprisingly, when the Austrian national team played its first game since the end of the Great War in 1919, Meisl lined up with nine of his 11 coming from SK Rapid. Some of the most recurrent names that SK Rapid lent to the national team in those years were the small but strong defender Vinzenz Dittrich, who teamed up with Josef 'Seppi' Brandstetter, the wide players Leopold Nitsch and Karl Wondrak and the devastating forward line consisting of Gustav Wieser, Richard Kuthan and Josef Uridil.

For Schönecker, everything was conditional on making SK Rapid the strongest team in Europe, a goal he would achieve in 1930 with his victory in the Mitropa Cup. In fact, Schönecker's success in the top competition of the time had come after defeat to Sparta in the first final, three years previously.

In 1930 the ride towards the title had presented no hiccups until the final. In the quarter-finals, SK Rapid had demolished Genoa – then called Genova 1893 Circolo di Calcio – thanks to the resounding 6-1 win in the home leg, and in the semi-finals the same fate fell to Ferencvaros, who were defeated 5-1 in Vienna. The final represented a chance for revenge after the 1927 event, as it put the green-and-whites once again in front of Sparta Prague, coached by Scotland's John Dick. This time the decisive match was the first leg, played away and finishing 2-0 to the Viennese. That was enough for the title despite a 3-2 defeat at home.

The good European results achieved by SK Rapid during those years were not unexpected. To some important players who had contributed to the successes of the previous years – such as Kuthan and Wondrak – had been added the likes of Karl Rappan, and midfielder and future coach of the Swiss national team, Josef Smistik, who represented the ideal type of central midfielder to be employed in the famous pyramid, the 2-3-5, thanks to his skill in recovering balls and restarting the action, and the prolific attackers Matthias Kaburek and Franz Weselik.

Schönecker's merits had also been immense from an economic point of view: he decided to build the Pfarrwiese, the club's first real stadium, in 1912, and was able to expand the number of fans by drawing on even the most affluent classes, such as doctors, artists and businessmen. A few years later, the club's finances had been restored and the stadium's capacity increased to 25,000 seats. He died in 1938 and was buried at Baumgarten Cemetery. Near today's Allianz Stadium a street, Schöneckerstrasse, was named after him and a statue dedicated to him stands just outside the stadium. His motto had always been, 'Those who stick together, win!' In 1999, the club decided to consult its fans in order to choose the best SK Rapid team of all time. In addition to Josef Uridil, the centre-forward who, more than any other, had been the club's most successful player during the amateur era, Franz Binder also appeared. Franz 'Bimbo' Binder, nicknamed as such because of his resemblance to a film actor of the time, is still considered one of the greatest Austrian players ever, having scored more than 1,000 goals (according to unofficial statistics) throughout his career.

He had arrived at SK Rapid from Sturm 19 in St Pölten and would never leave the green-and-white club from then on. Legend has it that Binder was able, thanks to his extraordinary shooting power, to break through opponents' goal nets.

The history of SK Rapid between the two wars is strongly linked to this man: thanks to Binder's feats, SK Rapid won the Austrian championship four times and the Austrian Cup once. He also triumphed in 1938, the year of the Anschluss, and in 1939 he won the Tschammerpokal, the then German Cup. He was also the main architect of Rapid's victory in the legendary 1941 final of the German inter-war championship, scoring three goals against Schalke 04 and contributing significantly to the 4-3 final.

Back in Vienna, the SK Rapid players were received by the mayor and SA-Gruppenführer Neubar at the capital's town hall. The party was incredible, even though the war was already under way. Thus, SK Rapid were the only Austrian team to triumph in all the top competitions organised by the Reich, and as the winner of the 1941 German championship, they temporarily received the Victoria, a cup which was donated by the DFB – German Football Association – to the winners of the German championship from 1903 to 1944. The trophy was named Victoria in honour of the Roman goddess of victory whose figure was represented on the cup.

During the Second World War, due to the unrest in Vienna, the cup passed into the hands of a Berlin citizen who hid it in his cellar under a pile of coal. Because of this, the Meisterschale – today's trophy – was created in 1949 with all the names of the previous winners. For 45 years it was thought that Victoria had been lost, but it was returned to the DFB after the fall of the Berlin Wall.

SK Rapid were the only non-commissioned team in the Federal Republic of Germany to win the Victoria. There was a strong feeling among the crowd that the final, held at the Olympic Stadium in Berlin, should have ended differently. Or rather, both in Vienna and in Germany, there was a rumour that the Reich leadership did not look favourably on the victory of an Austrian team in the German championship. There are two photos of the SK Rapid players on the sidelines, at the start of the match, immortalised as they greeted the fans in the stands. In one of them the Austrian players show the Nazi salute; in the other they don't. At the end of the war, when there was a return to the sporting events that had characterised that period, the photo with the SK Rapid players saluting was kept hidden. The club wanted to distance itself from its recent past, although today both photos are available to the public at the Rapideum, the SK Rapid museum. A few years earlier, in 1938, this was not the case: SK Rapid, like several other clubs in the capital, had decided to comply with the new government in office by claiming a National Socialist identity, although in fact the club had never been linked to a party. In spite of this, the fact that it was born as the Viennese workers' club made things easier from this point of view: many of its supporters were born and raised in the suburbs, which remained the basin within which the workers' movements gathered most of their support.

In Altreich, the term used to define Germany before 1938, SK Rapid were considered the most fearsome Viennese team and from that same year Franz Binder and other players of the club wore the German jersey on some occasions, although not everyone took part in the 1938 World Cup. Many, including

Skoumal, Pesser and Binder himself to name but a few, were summoned to the Wehrmacht.

Franz Binder was an important link for the club between the pre-war and post-war years: he was the manager of the green-and-whites from 1946 to 1951 and from 1962 to 1966, leading SK Rapid to three more national titles. He would then return to the club in 1976 with Robert Körner, winning the Austrian Cup.

A curious anecdote concerning Franz Binder was the transfer of one of the future stars of the team, defender Gerhard Hanappi, from Wacker Vienna. Hanappi wanted to play with SK Rapid but his club didn't want to let him leave. That's when Binder came into play, kidnapping the player and taking him to SK Rapid. Due to the illegitimacy of this transfer, Hanappi could not wear the Rapid shirt for six months. After that, he would become a legend of the club and the Austrian national team, finishing third in the 1954 World Cup.

# 3

FK AUSTRIA Vienna is one of the capital's two leading teams – the other, as noted, is First Vienna – whose roots go back to the English founding fathers. In 1894, Vienna Cricket and Football Club was born and in 1910, due to an internal split, gave birth to Wiener Cricket. The managers of the new club managed to convince some players to take up their cause, and from that day on the team's colours changed from the black and blue uniform initially adopted to white and purple, colours that still identify Favoriten's club.

But that same year, a new name change took place: Wiener Cricket did not excite anyone, and Die Veilchen – the Violets, as the supporters and players of Austria Vienna are nicknamed – changed their name to Wiener Amateur Sportverein. The following year the Amateure became part of the ÖFV.

The club distinguished itself from the very beginning for being – in contrast to SK Rapid – the team that best represented bourgeois Vienna and the Vienna of coffee houses, and several of its managers were part of the Jewish bourgeoisie.

Amateure, compared to other clubs that had arisen around the capital, boasted considerable economic strength that had allowed over the years the arrival of stars from nearby Hungary such as Alfred Schaffer and the Konrad brothers, Jenő and Kalman, transfers considered unusual at a time when football was still an amateur phenomenon. Moreover, it was well known that managers, fans and players of Amateure – among them Sindelar, a few years later – were frequent visitors to the coffee houses. While fans of SK Rapid met in the suburbs like those of other clubs, the supporters of FK Austria had a fixed meeting point: Café Parsifal, a café on the Ringstrasse, the area surrounding the city centre and the main tourist attractions. Gambling was frequent in these circles. It was rumoured that the managers of the team bet for hours, throwing 100 shillings at the table.

But strangely enough, even though the club had a lot of capital at its disposal, it would not have its own stadium for years. In the mid-1920s, the team played in the residential district of Ober St. Veit, not far from the SK Rapid pitch. But two months later the Great War broke out and the ground was abandoned without any maintenance being carried out. However, at the end of the First World War several matches were played on the Ober St Veit field, and when this was not possible the matches would be played on a neutral pitch.

The facilities in Ober St Veit hosted the Fussball Klub Austria – a name that the club would adopt from 28 November 1926 – until 1931, when the company that owned the land decided to raise the rent without agreeing with the club. The difficulty of adopting a regular and stable playing ground of its own led the club to play in 15 stadiums from the early days to 1982, the year in which it settled at the Franz Horr Stadium.

A peculiarity of the club that seemed evident long before the outbreak of the Great War was a certain aptitude to play international competitions: under the colours of Wiener Cricket and Football Club, they had in fact triumphed twice, between 1898 and 1902, in the Challenge Cup. The successes in the Challenge Cup had brought some of their favourites into the limelight: one of the first was Ludwig 'Luigi' Hussak, a forward, and scorer of the first official goal in the history of Vienna's Violets. Among other things, Hussak also scored a goal in the play-off for third and fourth place at the 1912 Olympics with the Austrian national team.

In those years, Amateure had begun to develop a refined style conceived by the minds of Jimmy Hogan and Hugo Meisl, who had coached the club between 1912 and 1914, the year in which Meisl was called up to the military. Later, the Hogan–Meisl duo would bring the same approach to the Austrian national team.

On a local level, however, the club's results were decidedly positive: between 1911 and 1923, Amateure established themselves as one of the main rivals of SK Rapid but never overhauled them and finished second three times. In order to contend for the title, the Hungarian star Alfred Schaffer was bought, and just a year later Amateure won their first national title.

Schaffer was one of those players who was either loved or hated. Bruno Kreisky, who would become Chancellor after the war, called him a great example. For others, however, he was a mercenary who didn't miss the opportunity to get an increase in his pay. Within a year, Schaffer had managed to double his salary. But it wasn't just Schaffer's purchase that strengthened the Amateure: that same year, another deadly attacker in the shape of Gustav Wieser had arrived. Before joining Amateure, Wieser had helped the fortunes of SK Rapid and Würzburger Kickers, and was another one of those purchases outside of the reach of most clubs.

Along with the national title, Amateure also won the Vienna Cup that year, a trophy that would later be renamed the Austrian Cup. The team was noteworthy for its attacking line-up, which in addition to Wieser and Schaffer also included Kalman Konrad, another formidable striker from Hungary.

These were years in which Amateure were unanimously considered one of the best central European teams, despite some important players having left the club. But at the same time Amateure had signed a rising star of Austrian football, Matthias Sindelar, who arrived with three other team-mates from Hertha Vienna, another of Favoriten's clubs from which Amateure used to draw the most promising talents.

In the 1925/26 season – after the success of Hakoah the previous year – Amateure won their first professional title, and the second in their history. Against the backdrop of the sporting successes, however, there were considerable economic difficulties that had developed since football had become professional. Now Amateure – like other teams in the capital – had to face additional costs and expenses corresponding to stadium maintenance, advertising investments, expenses for sports equipment and more. The *Neue Wiener Journal*, in an article entitled 'Budget of Viennese Football', argued that the new professional system had been launched too quickly and had brought a large number of teams to the brink of bankruptcy. In any case, winning the title had partly helped to cover up these difficulties.

Amateure were now characterised by their great ability to score goals, and one of their most influential players, Viktor Hierländer, said years later, 'We were the first to develop that game that would later go down in history as the Vienna School: a precise and close game with a completely exclusive charm.' Between 1926 and 1933, other teams contended for the title. Amateure's economic difficulties would worsen, leading Kalman Konrad – who returned after a brief interlude at First Vienna – to move to the United States, thus expanding the colony of Austro-Hungarian footballers who had already settled overseas for a couple of years. Sindelar had decided to stay instead, despite an important offer from SK Rapid. The club also found itself forced to lower its salaries, which in some cases fell below the ÖFB ceiling of 300 shillings.

On 28 November 1926 the club changed its name to Fussballklub Austria, commonly FK Austria. This decision was taken at the end of a members' meeting at the Dom Café. The main promoter of the initiative was Emanuel 'Michi' Schwarz, who, although he was to become president in 1932, already had some influence in the club. In addition, Schwarz, who was the director of Schwimmklub Austria at the time, wanted to give the club a name that would allow him to distance himself permanently from the now outdated amateur model.

These were, however, years in which the Violets were unable to repeat the sporting successes of previous years, despite Sindelar having definitively established himself as one of the main stars on the world scene. The transition seasons went on until 1933, when the club won the Winter Cup – the old Vienna Cup – now played according to the format of a championship. But despite many other farewells, one player remained: Matthias Sindelar, who in the meantime had refused yet another offer from Slavia Prague, the Czechs intending to replace their great centre-forward František Svoboda with the Austrian star. It was to the good fortune of FK Austria that they kept Sindelar, who won the Mitropa Cup twice.

The rules of the Mitropa Cup provided that each member country could decide whether to send its two best representatives – those who took first and second place in the championship – or the winner of the championship and the winner of the national cup to participate in the competition. The ÖFB had opted for the latter solution, and the club in Favoriten would definitely benefit from it.

The victory in the Mitropa Cup in 1932/33 was a confirmation of what had been a characteristic trend of the club up to that point: an innate propensity to play international competitions. After the successes of the first years in the Challenge Cup, when the team still bore the name of Vienna Cricket and Football Club, FK Austria also shone in the Mitropa Cup.

After seeing off Slavia Prague and Juventus, FK Austria had reached the final where they would find another Italian team in the shape of Ambrosiana di Meazza.

The first leg at the Arena Civica in Milan ended 2-1 for Ambrosiana, Spechtl's goal at the end of the match keeping the hopes of the Austrian side alive. The return match was played on 8 September 1933 in front of 58,000 spectators. The match – contested by Italian newspapers in the following days because of an refereeing decision considered unfair – ended 3-1 in favour of the Austrians thanks to Sindelar's hat-trick and FK Austria had won their first Mitropa Cup.

That victory improved the club's finances, and Schwarz – as he used to do – had awarded individual prizes to his players of 400 shillings for the passage to the quarter-finals, 500 for the qualification to the semi-finals and 1,000 if the team had brought home the cup.

In 1935 Jenő Konrad arrived at the club. He had coached FC Nürnberg and had come close to the German title, which he lost in the semi-finals against Bayern Munich. Despite his good results on the field, his stay in Nuremberg was marked by the repeated anti-Semitic abuse he had suffered. Some openly anti-Jewish newspapers, such as *Der Sturmer*, had harshly attacked him after his defeat against Bayern, Konrad had paid the price for the fact that Nuremberg had become one of the main National Socialist strongholds, and from 1927 had started to host several party assemblies.

Under Konrad's leadership, FK Austria won their second Mitropa Cup in 1936/37: after winning against Grasshoppers in the knockout round, Sindelar and his team-mates got the better of Bologna, Slavia Prague, Újpest and then Sparta Prague in the final.

However, 1937 was also a year of mourning for the Violets: Hugo Meisl – former manager and coach and founder of the cup in which the club had repeatedly distinguished itself – died of a heart attack. Also in the championship, FK Austria had finished tied on points with Admira but a worse goal difference had cost them the title.

Following the Anschluss, FK Austria were subjected to extraordinary administration: only a few days after the annexation, Hermann Haldenwang, an SA commander and former Amateure player, was appointed interim director. Haldenwang went so far as to prevent the players from greeting their former Jewish leaders, and the club's movable and immovable property was confiscated. Years later, Franz Schwarz, son of president Emanuel Schwarz, told the story:

'Suddenly, Haldenwang showed up and claimed to be the new club director. The first thing I noticed was how Haldenwang and our midfielder Johann Mock always showed up in their National Socialist uniforms. My father was expropriated a gold trophy that was a replica of the Mitropa Cup.'

For a few months, the club was forced to change its name to Ostmark – the same name by which the country itself had been renamed – and its Jewish leaders were forced to abandon their jobs and find refuge abroad. Emanuel Schwarz packed his bags to flee to the United States, but due to some bureaucratic hurdles he had to turn back to Italy: thanks to the help of the FIGC (Federazione Italiana Giuoco Calcio – the Italian Football Federation) he would first settle in

Bologna and then leave for Paris. There he would hide for the duration of the war. Ludwig 'Luigi' Hussak, the club's very first great star, also suffered the same fate. Norbert Lopper, a former player and club executive, fled to Belgium and was deported to Auschwitz in 1942. There he lost his wife, Rebecca, along with other relatives. Lopper was repeatedly tortured and sent to the Muthausen concentration camp in 1945, which fortunately for him was liberated in May of the same year. Robert Lang, coach of the club between 1928 and 1930, escaped to Yugoslavia but was captured and murdered in November 1941.

Instead of Schwarz – who was to return at the end of the war – came Bruno Eckerl, a lawyer, who would become a member of the National Socialist Party in 1941. Several players had fled because of the deteriorating situation: Camillo Jerusalem headed to France and returned to Vienna during the war years, while Walter Nausch went to Switzerland. Here he would take up the coaching career that would lead him to take charge of the Austrian team from 1948.

Nausch was able to give partial continuity to the Wunderteam legend: he trained players of the calibre of Stojaspal, Dienst, Körner, Ocwirk and Hanappi, finishing third in the 1954 World Cup. The war years were not favourable to Favoriten's club, which never triumphed in Gauliga Ostmark. And, deprived of the opportunity to compete in the competitions in which they had enjoyed success, the Austrian Cup and the Mitropa Cup, the club would occupy the role of an extra from there until the end of the war, when another generation of champions blossomed.

# 4

ADMIRA, AS well as SK Rapid, were born in one of the suburbs of the capital. From 1905 to 1971, the year in which they merged with Wacker Wien, they would have held their home fixtures in Floridsdorf, today a suburb of the capital that was an independent municipality at the time. More precisely, Admira Vienna was born around the Jedleseer Schwarzlackenau area thanks to members of the Sturm sports club, which had founded an association called Admira in 1897.

On 30 July 1899 the Ersten Groß-Floridsdorfer Fußballklub Admira was founded. The name Admira derives from a liner that brought one of the players home in 1897. Only four years later, however, the club ceased to exist but was reborn in 1905 with the same name following the merger with two other teams from the same district, Burschenschaft Einigkeit and SK Vindobona. For everyone, Admira Vienna would have been born at that time. In 1906 the club won its first trophy after a tournament in which five other teams from the capital participated.

Three years later, Admira moved to the outskirts of Pollak, another suburb of Floridsdorf which was home to an important textile district. Among the companies present in the district there was also Hermann Pollak's Sohne, situated along the then Jubiläumsgasse, today Deublergasse.

Of the four Viennese teams who dominated the championship until the return to amateur football, Admira had the slowest development. In the very early years of the 20th century, Admira were not one of the capital's leading teams and had never taken part in the Challenge Cup, unlike First Vienna, SK Rapid and Wiener Cricketer.

When the first Austrian championship began in 1911, Admira were not there. They were supposed to participate in the second championship, the 2. Klass, but were relegated to the fourth tier. This sanction was imposed after the club's top management had invited a team from Bratislava, Pressburger Torna-Elf, to play a match in Austria to favour a betting round. The rules prohibited certain matches and the team was ousted by the ÖFV.

Admira were, however, at a higher level than they would have faced in the years prior to its return to the top series. The year in which they played in the fourth division they scored 122 goals, conceding only eight, and in the following year, in the third division, they scored 88 and conceded 12.

The club began to cultivate even greater ambitions that would turn into results with the help of the surrounding factories. Its activities were financed by a number of local factories, including Hermann Pollak's Sohne, Mautner-Markhof, owner of the St Georgs-Brauerei beer brand, and Pauker, which built locomotives. The support of these giants had meant that, compared to other teams in the suburban districts whose social connotations were red or proletarian, Admira Vienna had assumed a less defined identity: it had been founded in the suburbs, but could not be defined in all respects as a working-class team.

In 1914, the club changed its name to Sportklub Admira Wien and at the end of the Great War, Admira became a permanent presence within the first division. The stadium was expanded to accommodate 10,000 spectators. The beginning, however, was disastrous: the players ended their first season in the highest division in last place and did not go down in the 2. Klass only because of the rules of those years that did not foresee promotions or relegations. They were slightly better the following year and finished second from bottom.

The 1922/23 season saw Admira finish third, the best position in their short history. Then, between 1927 and 1938, Admira lived their golden age, winning eight national titles and five Austrian Cups.

Three years before the first title, the chairmanship was taken by Rudolf Mütz, an executive of Hermann Pollak's Sohne who would remain in office until 1930 and then be elected honorary president. Under Mütz's leadership, Admira won two national titles – the first since they were founded – and finished second twice, also reaching the semi-final of the Mitropa Cup in 1928.

Before 1927, Admira had scarcely been on Hugo Meisl's radar and the coach had rarely selected their players for international games. When the first edition of the International Cup began, the presence of Admira's players in the Austrian national team's 11 regulars had become much more notable. Defenders Anton Janda and forwards Ignaz Siegl and Anton Schall became pillars of that team. Schall scored 231 goals in 285 games, five times finishing as the top scorer in the Austrian championship. At the end of his career, he died on a football pitch during a training session in Basel, where he was coaching.

Admira's winning cycle continued even after Mütz left the club's presidency: between 1930 and 1938, Admira won four more championships and two Austrian Cups, although in 1934 they were beaten by Bologna in the final of the Mitropa Cup.

The team was stronger than a few years previously. In addition to Schall, Admira included players of the calibre of Peter Platzer, Johann Urbanek, Adolf Vogl and Wilhelm Hahnemann, who were all a part of the Wunderteam at various points.

In 1938, following his return to amateur football, Rudolf Mütz, who continued to act as the club's financier, lost his job as director at Hermann Pollak's Sohne: the factory had been Aryanised by banks, and its owner Hans Grödel, a Jewish citizen, had been expropriated. The fact that Mütz had converted to Christianity at the age of 20 was not enough for the National Socialists: the persecution would have involved him too. At the time, a Jewish citizen living under the Reich still had an opportunity to emigrate but to do so, however, he had to pay the *Reichsfluchtsteuer*, a tax to which other German and Austrian citizens who wanted to leave the motherland were also subject. Mütz paid 47,000 German marks and fled to Yugoslavia, just as Josef Gerö, president of the Vienna Football Association, and Robert Lang, former coach of Austria Vienna, did the same. Mütz died as a result of the Nazi occupation of Yugoslavia in 1943, as did Lang, while Gerö survived.

Admira won the 1939 championship, the first since football had become amateur. As the winner of the Gauliga Ostmark, Admira took part in the German championship and made it to the final, but they suffered a heavy and surprising 9-0 defeat by Schalke 04.

The dominant feeling among Admira fans and more generally among Austrian supporters was that the match had been spoiled by biased refereeing. Anton Schall and Peter Platzer, two of the players who had been part of the Wunderteam during the 1934 World Cup, had not taken to the pitch. A week earlier they had won the Reichsbund Cup

Final in the Ostmark jersey against Silesia, and had suffered injuries. Instead of Platzer, in came Buchberger, a very young goalkeeper who had also come to the match after nine months of service at the Wehrmacht. Years later, Buchberger would confess that he had been under a lot of pressure: at only 18 years old, playing the third match of his career in front of almost 100,000 opposing fans had not been easy at all. Moreover, Admira were left with ten men due to the dismissal of Fritz Klacl. The Austrian midfielder had spoken badly to the German centre-forward Fritz Szepan, and in the 52nd minute he had knocked Szepan out, leaving him bleeding on the ground. The referee had no doubts and sent Klacl off, allowing Schalke 04 to go on and extend their already healthy lead.

That match was the instigator of increasing scuffles at stadiums whenever an Austrian team faced German opposition. The following year a friendly was organised in Vienna between the two teams but it saw violent clashes between fans before, during and afterwards. Some newspapers tried to play it down by focusing on the highlights of the game, while others, such as *Völkischer Beobachter*, claimed that it was 'the darkest day in the history of Viennese football, a day to forget'.

However, the story had little prominence in the newspapers: Adolf Hitler had forbidden any mention of the conflicts between Ostmark and Altreich, even when they took place in sport. Moreover, after the police intervened, the Viennese National Socialist leaders were convinced that the situation would calm down. Those who paid for the scuffles were 220 mostly teenage Viennese fans who were sent to labour camps and psychiatric institutions.

From that moment until the end of the war, Admira would no longer be among the top four teams of Gauliga Ostmark.

The team even ended up being relegated and would return to the top division in the 1942/43 season, thanks above all to the feats of Franz Konecny, a player who had faked an injury so as not to be summoned to the war front.

Admira won the championship and cup again in 1966, and in 1971 they merged with Wacker Wien, taking the name Admira Wacker.

# V

# TOUCHING EUROPE'S ROOF: THE FIRST WUNDERTEAM AND THE INTERNATIONAL CUP

*According to historians, there was a first and a second Wunderteam. They were very different teams that had, however, two common denominators: Hugo Meisl and Matthias Sindelar, in addition to the famous pyramid module. The first Wunderteam started in 1931 after a 5-0 victory against Scotland which earned Meisl's team the nickname that would accompany it in the following years and ended with a victory in the International Cup (or Antonin Švehla Cup). The second was the one that saw Austria arrive as favourites at the 1934 World Cup with Sindelar who had reached a state of full maturity. Overall, Austria achieved two impressive sequences of results: the first started with the victory on 12 April 1931 in the International Cup match against Czechoslovakia and was interrupted by the defeat in the friendly against England in 1932; and the second, of 12 matches, culminated in the semi-final of the 1934*

*World Cup against Italy. That defeat, considered by many as a handover between the strongest team of the first half of the 1930s and the best of the second, was in fact only one of many chapters of a rivalry that had begun years earlier and would continue for years to come. A rivalry in which football, politics and propaganda would be inextricably linked.*

# 1

THE CONSEQUENCES of the Great War, at the end of which the Austro-Hungarian Empire had been dissolved, giving rise to a patchwork of countries formed for the first time in the form of republics, would also have reverberated around the world of football. The Treaty of Trianon, signed by the victorious powers, had drastically reduced the territory of what had been the Kingdom of Hungary, while the treaties of Versailles and Saint-Germain-en-Laye had limited the borders of Austria and Germany and had prohibited the formation of a pan-Germanic empire composed of the two nations.

The crisis was spreading and issues such as recession or unemployment immediately became apparent. Some articles of the Treaty of Saint-Germain-en-Laye had also emphasised the protection of the rights of ethnic minorities, obliging Austria to guarantee freedom of religion, to recognise Austrian nationality for any person born on Austrian territory and equality before the law for any citizen, regardless of his or her ethnicity or religion. The clauses imposed by the Treaty of Saint-Germain-en-Laye, although they did not eliminate certain problems such as anti-Semitism or discrimination against minorities, nevertheless had the effect of forcing the government to take an official position to combat these problems. It is no coincidence that, before and after the unrest in Hungary since the rise to power of Miklos Horthy, a former admiral known for his anti-Semitic and anti-communist ideas, Vienna had remained the main landing place for the Hungarian community that had decided to expatriate.

The Hungarians who had settled in Austria at the end of the First World War had numbered around 100,000, most of them Jews and, both during the years of the Socialist Republic of Kun and during the following years under Horthy, were political opponents. One of them, in 1919, was Gyula Gömbös, who would become Horthy's right-hand man a few years later.

The problems most felt, however, remained the crisis and unemployment. And the violence had not disappeared at all. In May 1919, the Austrian Conservative newspaper *Innsbrucker Nachrichten* pointed out that the end of the Great War had not in fact helped to make Europe a more peaceful and secure place. In fact, a series of paramilitary organisations had blossomed and would sow terror and violence until 1923, mainly composed of men who had particularly suffered the consequences of the defeat and who came mostly from the multi-ethnic and infamous suburbs of the big cities or from more isolated villages.

Subsequent analyses would have shown that the following enjoyed by National Socialism was particularly rooted in these territories. In general, there was a strong resentment towards the victorious powers who, besides having redefined the borders of the defeated nations, had emptied their already-devastated coffers by imposing heavy economic sanctions.

International relations between European countries in the inter-war period went hand in hand with sporting relations. For years, relations remained frozen. Between 1918 and 1922, Austria only played friendlies against teams from countries alongside which it had fought at the front or which had taken a neutral position, such as Switzerland and Sweden. In 1922, for the first time, Austria returned to play against an inveterate nation only a few years earlier: Italy. By the end of 1920, in fact, it was Italy who had broken the ice by inviting an Austrian team to play a friendly on their own soil.

In Hungary, the key figure in this regard was the diplomat Mór Fischer, who organised several friendlies with foreign teams in the 1920s. In 1929, facilitated by the various bilateral agreements that Mussolini and Minister Grandi had closed with Austria and Hungary, the Italian clubs had begun to take part in the Mitropa Cup, which had begun only two years earlier.

Relations between the nations of Europe had definitely changed from a few years earlier, and from 1933 onwards they were practically reversed: Italy and Austria, for example, formed an alliance to protect Austria's borders from an invasion by Hitler's Germany. By 1924, sporting relations had taken a similar turn: Germany had requested the expulsion of Austria from FIFA when it joined professional football, and in 1927, when the Mitropa Cup and the International Cup were founded, the DFB, although invited to participate in the International Cup, did not accept because it did not want to compete with professional players.

International Cup, in reality, was just the name that the event would take on in Italy. Officially, the cup had been named Coupe Internationale Européenne, but each country used a different title. In Austria it was the Europapokal, in Hungary the Europá Kupa and in Czechoslovakia the Mezinárodní Póhar.

Until 1938, European football at the highest levels had been reserved for some of the former powers of the Austro-Hungarian Empire, such as Austria, Hungary and Czechoslovakia, and Italy, because Germany was excluded from it and England persisted in its sports isolationism.

The assumptions on which the International Cup was born were the same on which the Mitropa Cup was founded: the will and the need for clubs and federations to collect money so that they could earn and meet the increased expenses foreseen by the professional model. In reality, the Mitropa Cup and the International Cup would have been in some way competing tournaments: the International Cup was organised in a format similar to that of a league with home and away matches, and it was not uncommon for a player's presence in an International Cup match to affect his or her availability for a league or Mitropa Cup fixture. In most cases, however, clubs were able to keep their players from being called up to the national team.

Both the Mitropa Cup and the International Cup were born thanks to the resourcefulness of Hugo Meisl. While the international friendlies at the time already attracted a large number of spectators – although fewer than they would have attracted since 1927, when the first edition of the International Cup was held – the same could not be said of the friendlies between club teams. It was after one of these matches that Meisl realised how important it was to restructure international football. The friendly between First Vienna and Slavia Prague, technically a high-profile encounter, had only attracted 3,000 spectators.

Like the Mitropa Cup, the International Cup was conceived in 1926, during a conference held in Prague, but compared to the Mitropa Cup, whose revenue would go into the pockets of the clubs, the International Cup would benefit the federations of the nations involved. In any case, the objective was the same: to fill the stadiums as much as possible.

Initially, however, the Prague conference had aroused much scepticism among some of the participating federations, such as the Dutch, English, French and Belgians. In December 1926 a second conference was held, this time in Paris, at the end of which the plan to establish the International Cup was rejected. Decisive in arriving at the definition of the International Cup was the conference held in 1927 where Meisl, supported by Henri Delaunay – who, like the Austrian coach, would also play an important role in the creation of the World Cup – proposed a new plan to FIFA which was finally approved. A committee was appointed and the International Cup was officially born, although in fact it was, contrary to Meisl's hopes, a cup almost exclusively reserved for the nations of central Europe.

In July 1927, one day apart, the first conferences for the Mitropa Cup and the International Cup were organised in Venice. It was decided that each edition of the International Cup should last for two years, and that the competition for professionals would be accompanied by a second one for amateur teams. In reality, the difficulties for the national teams and clubs to get their commitments together – especially since other events emerged – meant that some editions lasted for a longer period of time.

The cup was also named Švehla Cup, in honour of Antonín Švehla, the then Czechoslovak Prime Minister who decided to donate a crystal cup as a prize for the winner. Despite this, the most common name in the press would have been the European Cup, a name that best summed up the nature of the event. The creation of the International Cup – simultaneously or almost simultaneously with the Mitropa Cup – was yet another success for Hugo Meisl. Italy's Mario Ferretti was appointed president, despite the fact that his nation's teams would not initially take part in the Mitropa Cup. They started competing from 1929, when the first national championship was born in Italy. Meisl maintained his position as secretary and for both the Mitropa Cup and the International Cup a council was established in Vienna, along the Tegethoffstrasse.

The numbers of spectators testified to the success of the event. While a friendly between Austria and Switzerland in 1926 had attracted 19,000 people, two years later, the crowd had doubled for an International Cup match. The audience would have grown in proportion to the popularity of the Austrian line-up, and would have reached the highest peaks since 1931, when Austria had become the Wunderteam for everyone.

# 2

THE FIRST edition – held between 1927 and 1930 – was won by Vittorio Pozzo's Italy, with Austria and Czechoslovakia coming in joint second place. The rivals had scored the same amount of goals and had also conceded the same.

Before the competition began, Italy and Austria were the favourites. If in the early 1920s Italy and Austria had improved their institutional relations, between 1925 and 1926, an era in which Mussolini would intensify his progression of fascism, relations between the two countries had definitely cooled down. Austria, through its government, was fulfilling the obligations imposed on it by the victorious powers following the defeat in the Great War regarding the protection of minorities, while Italy, on the other hand, had begun to 'Italianise' those regions where there was a strong presence of linguistic and cultural minority, such as South Tyrol, where a large community lived whose main language was German.

Mussolini's politics sparked fierce protests in Austria. The ÖFB refused to take part in the congress of the federations the following May and in response the FIGC – now part of the fascist state – declared that the move 'truncated in the most complete way any relationship with the federation'. Not only that, the FIGC went on to add 'the gesture of Latin kindness that Italy would have made in returning to play after the Great War meetings with the defeat of Austria', and again emphasised the 'inviolable Italianity of Alto Adige', threatening to remove from its headquarters any reference to international meetings against Austria, such as photos or pennants.

Italy and Austria were to return to face each other on 6 November 1927 in the new and futuristic Littoriale Stadium in Bologna – opened just a few months earlier – in the International Cup. Despite the broken relations between the two nations and their respective federations, there were no clashes or tensions of any kind on the pitch.

A friendly played in 1929 at the Hohe Warte Stadium in Vienna, which ended 3-0 to the Austrians, would have caused more controversy. The Italians, the only ones who did not recognise the superiority of their rivals, would have pointed the finger at the hardness of the Austrians following a serious injury to one of their players, Janni.

In a context in which the rivalry between the two countries took on political as well as sporting connotations, Italian newspapers did not fail to point out some logistical problems that had occurred, such as an Italian flag hoisted with the tricolour arranged horizontally – a flag more similar to the Hungarian one – or the fact that the band in charge of playing the national anthems would replace the Royal March of Savoy with an Italian song chosen at random (an Italian newspaper claimed it was 'Santa Lucia').

In the middle of a fascist dictatorship, defeat was not allowed. All the more so when it was against a nation considered inferior, defeated years earlier on the battlefields. In the days following the meeting, the newspapers did not miss the opportunity to go over what happened in the Great War. One of them wrote that Austria had lost 'quite another match ten years ago when not only two teams, but two peoples, with their strength and traditions, were armed against each other'. Similar invectives also came from other newspapers, such as *Il Piccolo di Trieste*, founded under the Austro-Hungarian Empire, which with its words testified how the press were now enslaved to the fascist regime.

That the climate between the two nations had become red-hot was also leaked abroad: the *Deutsche Presse*, a German newspaper based in Prague, pointed out that even after the 11 battles of the Soča, Italy had not allowed itself to insult Austria so severely, despite the fact that Italy was not yet fascist at the time.

That edition of the International Cup had not started well for Austria, who had lost the first two matches against Czechoslovakia and Hungary, and were facing an uphill challenge. They did then beat Italy 1-0 at home and picked up four other victories. The competition had, however, highlighted a closeness between the participating teams. With the exception of Switzerland, who had finished with no points, the other four teams were barely separated. Italy came first with 11, Austria and Czechoslovakia followed with ten and Hungary came third with nine.

The fact that the competition took place over several years gave Hugo Meisl the opportunity to experiment with various formations, depending on the fitness of his players and the results achieved with their club sides. Matthias Sindelar, who was 24 years old at the time, was also one of the players called up but he was only used on one occasion, against Switzerland. It is fair to think that Sindelar's emergence into the Austrian national team was delayed by the disappointing results of Austria Vienna, who between 1926/27 and 1930/31 finished no higher than fifth. These were years in which SK Rapid and Admira dominated the Austrian championship, which is why Meisl mainly preferred players from these two clubs.

The friendlies played while the competition was going on were used instead to test new players. In the Mitropa Cup, Austria was represented by SK Rapid, who in 1927 and 1928 reached the final, losing to Sparta Prague and Ferencváros respectively and couldn't even have the chance to take part in World Cup that would be hosted in Uruguay in 1930 as the national sides of Austria, Hungary and Czechoslovakia were not represented. During those years, the central European clubs had no other showcase in which they could compete. Their players had been precluded from participating in the Olympic Games since the countries switched to professional football, and the first World Cup would take place in 1930, but these teams were not represented.

# 3

FROM 1930, Austrian football matured considerably. Starting in 1929, Italian teams also began to participate in the Mitropa Cup but in 1930 and 1931 it was two Austrian teams that won the leading European competition for club teams, SK Rapid and First Vienna.

As in the previous edition of the International Cup, the abundance of talent on the central European scene in those years made it difficult to establish a likely winner. However, the bitterest rivalry remained between Italy and Austria. In that edition of the International Cup, Italy against Austria would also have meant Giuseppe Meazza against Matthias Sindelar. The Italian, though very young, had been the top scorer in the previous Mitropa Cup and would soon become a key point of reference for his national team, while Sindelar would be definitively feted during the second edition of the International Cup.

But at the San Siro in Milan, Italy beat Meisl's men 2-1. Once again, triumphalism characterised the comments in Italian newspapers. At the end of the match, Vittorio Pozzo said, 'I feel like crying. We did it this time. We beat the unbeatable Austria after 20 years. We achieved the feat that had been attempted in vain by four generations of our best players.'

The Austrians' performances were up and down and their 2-1 victory against Czechoslovakia was followed by a dull 0-0 against Hungary in Vienna. It was just after the draw in the Danube derby that the press insisted that Meisl give Matthias Sindelar a chance alongside First Vienna's centre-forward Fritz Gschweidl. Meisl gave in, and Sindelar was included in the 11 to face Scotland in a friendly on 16 May 1931. Starting from that victory, Meisl could no longer ignore the FK Austria star who, after having contributed to humiliating Germany in two friendly matches, became an indispensable player in all subsequent matches of the International Cup.

After the 2-2 draw in Budapest against Hungary and the heavy 8-1 victory against Switzerland, it was again time for the great classic: Austria against Italy, this time in Vienna.

While the political invective continued in the newspapers, on the pitch the spotlight was particularly on Sindelar and Meazza. The teams gathered and the Italian line-up was whistled by the 60,000 spectators as soon as the players in blue jerseys showed the fascist salute.

Then the match began, and the two star men did not disappoint. Sindelar came out on top against Meazza and scored twice to secure the victory for Austria. 'Der Papierene' (the Paper Man, Sindelar's nickname) had highlighted his technical skills, with his goals coming from a pure centre-forward's header and a precision finish after a move that started in the middle of the field, separated by three minutes. By virtue of that draw, Austria led the table with Italy in second. Czechoslovakia were further back having fallen to a surprise defeat to Switzerland, who still finished at the bottom. It was clear that the champions would either be Austria or Italy.

They both had two games left to play. In the penultimate one, on 22 May 1932 in Prague against Czechoslovakia, which coincided with Karl Sesta's debut, Austria earned a 1-1 draw. Even the challenge between the two most influential players had ended level: František Svoboda had responded to Sindelar's header.

In their final match, Austria got the better of Switzerland with a 3-1 win, although the performance was harshly criticised by the home crowd. By the 1930s, Viennese spectators had developed a taste for football that went far beyond just the result. Therefore, a victory that was not accompanied by a good performance was challenged. All in all, even Meisl had not hidden his dissatisfaction, claiming that his team had a bad day.

The mood of the press reflected that of the supporters. *Das Kleine Blatt,* for example, wrote that the public's protests would be directed more at the coach than at the team, while *Neue Freie Presse* wrote of 'a victory too small for 55,000 spectators'. *Reichpost* instead pointed the finger at the team's physical fitness, which the newspaper said was inadequate.

But despite this, Italy's defeat against Czechoslovakia in Prague handed the title to Meisl's men. Because of that victory, the following year the Wunderteam were invited to play a friendly match in England against the English national side. It was an honour bestowed on very few teams.

4

THE THIRD edition of the International Cup, running from 1933 to 1935, had two peculiarities: it took place during a period in which its popularity had faded, and it saw the relations between the usual main contenders, Austria and Italy, change radically.

Unlike in 1930, all the major nations of continental Europe were to take part in the second edition of the World Cup in 1934, the first held in Europe. This had led the public to focus their attention on a more inclusive event, and from that moment on the International Cup was seen by many as a sort of smaller World Cup.

The third edition of the International Cup began only a few months after Adolf Hitler's ascent to power in Germany. The theme of the Anschluss had returned to the agenda, and although it was forbidden by the treaties signed after the Great War, it received the approval of the Austrian National Socialist Party as well as support from Germany. Moreover, it was clear that Hitler was not in the least interested in respecting the institutional commitments imposed on Germany at the end of the First World War.

Two months after Hitler came to power, Austrian Chancellor Engelbert Dollfuss banned the Social Democratic Party and the National Socialist Party from the Austrian Parliament, and in May of the same year he created an era called Austrofascism, founding the Vaterländische Front, whose slogan was 'Wake Austria!' In February 1934, a violent civil war broke out between Linz and Vienna involving Social Democrats and government militias. Dollfuss managed to quell the rebellion, but on 25 July 'Millimetternich', as the Austrian Chancellor was nicknamed because of his short stature and outstanding diplomatic skills, lost his life following a coup organised and unsuccessfully completed by a group of members of the Austrian National Socialist Party who had raided the Chancellery.

The deadly blow had come from the hand of Otto Panetta, who confessed his responsibility for the death but not the intention to murder Dollfuss: according to him, the blow was accidental. But the court found that the defence was considered improbable, and at that point Panetta decided to rectify his version: he had acted out of personal revenge, since he attributed to Dollfuss his expulsion from the army years before. Kurt Alois von Schuschnigg took his place.

Since Hitler had come to power, an anti-German-style alliance had been formed between Mussolini and the Austrian Chancellor. After the death of Dollfuss, Italy had undertaken to deploy its troops on the Brenner Pass to protect itself against a possible German invasion of Austria, and in a bulletin Mussolini, as well as saying he was sorry for the death of the Austrian Chancellor, reiterated Italy's commitment to working with Austria.

On a sporting level, however, the competition was more interesting than ever. The Austrian Wunderteam, champions of the previous event, were in their prime, and 1933, the year in which the competition began, had seen an Austrian club, Austria Vienna, triumph in the Mitropa Cup. Italy, for its part, soon began a cycle that led them to triumph in the Olympic Games and twice in the World Cup. If Hungary in the early years had suffered a few shortcomings compared to the other European big names, Czechoslovakia would bring one of their two leading clubs, Sparta Prague, to triumph in the Mitropa Cup in 1935.

Despite the superior media attention paid to the World Cup matches, the International Cup continued to register very high attendances, as evidenced by the match between Italy and Austria played at the Mussolini Stadium in Turin, the largest in Italy, where there were 55,000 paying spectators. In no other Italian stadium would it have been possible to host such an event.

That match was Austria's first in the competition that year, while Italy had already played four times and were top of the standings with maximum points. Despite the absence of Matthias Sindelar, the Wunderteam won 4-2, with a hat-trick scored by Karl Zischek. Instead of Sindelar, in came Franz Binder, a very young forward who had only debuted for the national team the previous year in a friendly against Belgium. He had already started to make his mark for his club, SK Rapid, and scored the other goal for the Austrians. It was a reult of a quick attack with exchanges between Bican, debutant Kaburek and Viertl, a combination that made it clear that the Wunderteam were able to show their best moves despite the absence of several key players.

Hugo Meisl's choices were also backed up in the following match against Switzerland with Sindelar and Bican doing well, as did Binder and Kaburek. Austria won, but at 3-2 it was more challenging than they had expected. Bican scored twice and proved his coach's decision to be correct. Sindelar, now into his 30s, was still suffering from his annoying knee ache.

Meisl's experiments were not only important for the International Cup; the coach was also considering a technical revolution for the World Cup. The idea of discarding Sindelar, moreover, was not definitive. Sindelar reappeared in the starting 11 in the friendly against Hungary, which was won 5-2. Although he didn't score, the Austria Vienna star was a threat throughout and was to become one of the regular starters in the World Cup.

On 14 October 1934 – four months after the World Cup had ended – Austria returned to their International Cup fixtures, but suffered a disappointing 2-2 draw home against Czechoslovakia. Although the Czechoslovaks had been runners-up in the World Cup, the newspapers were outraged at the setback. The feeling was that the Wunderteam era was on the wane. Austria had lost the opportunity to close the gap to Italy in the table and the nation's newspapers, already outraged by the defeat in the World Cup semi-finals, could not contemplate a second Italian victory in another international competition.

Further eroding Austria's hopes of defending the title won the previous year was a 3-1 defeat against Hungary. At 2-1, the Austrians had complained about a disallowed goal by Sindelar. The referee had whistled for offside but Meisl's players were convinced that he had made the wrong decision. The newspapers instead did not look for excuses: they attacked the team and did not fail to emphasise Sindelar's poor form, claiming that he needed to rest and that he lacked dynamism.

About a month later, the Wunderteam – for some, the former Wunderteam – beat Switzerland 3-0 in their last match of 1934, a year that had been very intense and exhausting.

On 24 March 1935 in Vienna, Italy and Austria, separated by one point with the Italians just ahead, prepared for a decisive match. It should have taken place on 17 February, but since it was the anniversary of the previous year's civil war, the Austrian Chancellery had decided to postpone it until the following month. From Italy the fans flocked in en masse, while the Austrian authorities raised concerns about possible anti-Austrian and anti-Italian demonstrations organised by the National Socialists. Such disturbances did not occur, despite police reports that members of the then illegal SA had bought as many as 12,000 tickets. According to these reports, the operation was financed by Berlin, and in addition to launching rockets to form a giant swastika flag shortly before the match, it also involved members of the left, also against the Austrian government.

But none of these concerns materialised. The danger was averted despite six arrests caused by whistles to some officers of the Heimwehr, the Austrian paramilitary group. The Italian victory – thanks to goals by Ferrari and Piola – was a big step towards winning the competition. They led the table with ten points while Austria were behind them on seven. Austria drew their last two matches, 0-0 against Czechoslovakia in Prague and 4-4 against Hungary in Vienna. Italy, despite collecting only one point in the two remaining matches, kept their advantage and won a second International Cup.

In Italy the victory attracted political interest to the same degree as the World Cup won the previous year. The day after the 4-4 draw between Austria and Hungary, an Italian newspaper highlighted the presence in the stands of representatives of the three fascist nations, such as Mussolini's daughter, Countess Edda Ciano, the Hungarian representatives, Ugo Meisl – deliberately or erroneously written without the initial H – and Dr Eberstallen – instead of Eberstaller – without ever mentioning the members of the Czech and Swiss delegations. Ironically, Meisl proposed to rename that competition the Mussolini Cup.

# 5

THE LAST edition before the outbreak of the Second World War presented the same scenario: four of the strongest teams in the world competing for the title of the best European nation. The Wunderteam, however, had started to suffer a downturn in its fortunes. Meisl had argued that the Austrian national team needed to be refreshed, but that it would take time.

Meisl's experiments in the two friendly matches prior the start of the competition included a young attack line composed of Bican, Binder, and Hahnemann – 'The Gypsy', as he was nicknamed for his somatic traits, although in reality he came from a purely Viennese family – and more experienced players such as Smistik, Sesta, Zischek and Urbanek. Matthias Sindelar no longer appeared; Meisl had decided it was time for him to hang up his boots too.

On a political level, Hitler's expansionist aims towards neighbouring Austria had begun to undermine the political climate in Vienna. Moreover, from 1936 onwards, Italian support for Austria's independence had begun to falter. The previous year, Mussolini had begun to divert his attention to foreign policy issues, and on 5 May 1936, Badoglio arrived in Addis Ababa, ending the colonial war in Ethiopia.

Austria began with a 1-1 home draw against Czechoslovakia, followed two weeks later by a 5-3 defeat against Hungary in Budapest, where Bican scored his last international goal.

Between the defeat against Hungary and the third match against Switzerland there were two friendlies: the luxury encounter against the English, offering a chance for some sort of revenge after the meeting four years earlier, and one against Italy. Meisl recalled Sinderlar and used him in both of the friendlies.

On 8 November 1936, Austria played their third match against Switzerland and recorded their first victory. It was Hugo Meisl's last competitive match, and his penultimate in total. Meisl died on 17 February 1937, less than a month after the friendly against France. In the absence of Meisl, the manager of the national team before a successor was hired was ÖFB president Richard Eberstaller. He selected the 11 to face Italy on 21 March in Vienna.

After a minute of silence in memory of Meisl, a real battle began. Bad weather had arrived in Vienna and the crowd was upset about the delay in the match. After the first half-hour had passed without incident, the match became heated. Numerous hard challenges on both sides were due partly to the conditions of the pitch and partly, according to both Austrian and Italian sources, to the inadequacy of the Swedish referee, Olsson.

After a period of Austrian superiority, during which they opened the scoring, the Italians did not hold back and a brawl began that went on for a few minutes after Austrian scorer Jerusalem was kicked by Andreolo. Returned to the field after receiving treatment, Jerusalem took revenge off the ball and kicked Serantoni, leading to his dismissal. Before the second half began, the referee had threatened to abandon the match if the two teams did not calm down.

The battle, however, resumed and began to involve the fans too: the Italian supporters, after being surrounded and insulted, started to chant aggressively. In the 18th minute of the second half Austria doubled their lead. Colaussi – whose Trieste surname Colàusig had been Italianised – was fouled in the penalty area and Stroh scored to make it 2-0.

The bad challenges then continued with a charge on the Italian goalkeeper Olivieri and another foul by Colaussi on Stroh, so the referee abandoned the match. It was the first time in history that an international had been suspended before the final whistle. The clashes on the pitch subsided but they continued in the stands, and in fact hostilities between Austrian and Italian fans had started long before the referee blew the whistle at the start of the match: Italian supporters had railed against Viennese passers-by from the coaches accompanying them to the stadium, and at the end of the match some of them were blocked by Austrian supporters. Among the Italians who were stopped were 105 Trieste supporters who had come in support of Baron Albori, who had fought with opposing fans during the match and were then attacked by an elderly lady armed with an umbrella. Escorted by the police, the Italians – 16 of whom had been injured – finally managed to leave Vienna.

Albori, back in Italy, wrote a letter to the Italian ambassador in Vienna, Francesco Salata, in which he denounced the behaviour of the police, who he said were unable to maintain order and safeguard the safety of Italian fans.

At the same time as the battle of Guadalajara was being fought in Spain, which saw the Italian Fascist militias come to the rescue of the Francoist rebels and come out with broken bones, Vienna was full of people who took the opportunity to underline the similarities between the sporting and military defeat suffered by Fascist Italy. The lawyer Valentin Gelber, of socialist and anti-fascist extraction, printed 500 pamphlets entitled *Die Schlacht von Guadalajara im Wiener Stadion*, or

*The Battle of Guadalajara in the Vienna Stadium,* which were then sold in bookshops without being censored.

The federation decided that the match should be replayed, but the Austrians, feeling robbed of a deserved victory, refused. It was therefore expunged and no points were awarded. It would have been the last fixture between Italy and Austria before the Anschluss.

However, the rivalry continued in the Mitropa Cup. Towards the end of the first leg match between Genoa 1893 Cricket and Football Club – the current Genoa – and Admira, the Austrians were given a penalty which sent the Italians into a frenzy. Anger and nervousness took over and one of Genoa's players, Morselli, found himself with a triple jaw fracture.

Mussolini forbade the return match, but the Viennese team were only informed of this decision when they arrived in Klagenfurt. The Austrians reached Venice anyway, in the hope of the Duce's repentance. But it was in vain and they were ordered to leave Italy within 24 hours.

Before the Anschluss intervened, the Austrian national team played three more matches in the International Cup, collecting a 4-3 victory against Switzerland and two defeats against Hungary and Czechoslovakia.

The last game before the suspension of the tournament was Switzerland v Czechoslovakia on 3 April 1938. The tournament ended prematurely with Hungary in the lead, followed a point further back by Italy, but with three more matches left to play.

The Nazi invasion of Austria, moreover, had prevented the federations of Italy and Austria from strengthening their relations. A friendly match between the two teams was organised for the autumn of 1938 aimed at forgetting the unrest in Vienna and Genoa, but this never happened because Austria no longer existed in the autumn of 1938.

While the International Cup was abruptly interrupted, the Mitropa Cup would continue for another two years without the participation of the Austrian sides, although initially there were thoughts that the teams of the newborn Ostmark could take part or that the competition could be extended to German clubs. However, the DFB, true to the principles of amateur football, had refused. It had stressed that it did not want to take part in a competition 'invented by a Jew'.

Curiously enough, the 1938 edition of the Mitropa Cup, the first in history without Austrian representation, was won by Slavia Prague, dragged along by the goals of a player who only a couple of years earlier was wearing the white jacket of the Austrian national team: Josef Bican.

In 1948 the International Cup was restarted for two more editions. The format and the contenders had not changed, although these last two competitions lasted substantially longer than the previous ones. What had changed substantially was the quality of the European players taking part. One of them, a young Ferenc Puskás, contributed ten goals in the 1948–53 tournament, which represented Hungary's only overall victory.

The last edition – in which Yugoslavia also participated – was renamed the Dr Gerö Cup, in honour of the former president of the Vienna Football Association, who had become president of the ÖFB after the end of the Second World War and had died a year before that edition began. It was played between 1955 and 1960 and was won by Czechoslovakia, although one historical event had a decisive influence on its progress: Hungary, who had come second after the Hungarian Revolution of 1956, had lost several of their key players who had contributed to their 1948–1953 victory and who only two years previously had gone close to winning the World Cup. The best known, Puskás, Czibor and Kocsis, had found refuge in Spain where they would star for Real Madrid and Barcelona.

It was the last edition of the International Cup and was the forerunner to today's European Championship, more inclusive and having, at least in their first edition, a knockout format without groups. The idea was started by Henri Delaunay, who had been appointed UEFA's general secretary in 1954 and who had been dreaming together with Hugo Meisl since 1927 of creating a European competition in which all the national teams of the continent would participate. However, Delaunay died the following year and was unable to attend the first European Championship in 1960.

# VI

# MATTHIAS SINDELAR: THE MOZART OF FOOTBALL

*The Viennese football tradition had been churning out champions ever since the days when the English had imported the sport to the Austrian capital. After the early years, some Austrian players had started to appear for the main local clubs alongside their British colleagues from whom they would learn endlessly. Soon they would create a national team that would become the strongest in the Austro-Hungarian Empire and one of the most successful teams of the time. The first favourites of what was then a small audience were Ludwig Hussak and Johann Studnicka, symbols of Vienna Cricket and Football Clubs and WAC, the most successful clubs of the time. Then there was Josef Uridil, the Tank, the prolific striker for SK Rapid. Finally came Matthias Sindelar, at a time when football fever had broken out in Vienna thanks to the emergence of some international competitions. The prevailing feeling among the fans was that of being faced with a unique player, different from all the others. Alfred Polgar, one of the greatest exponents of Austrian modernism, had* said of him, 'He played football as a chess master moves his pawns, with such an extensive vision that he could calculate moves and counter moves in advance, always choosing the best of the options. He had unparalleled ball control combined with the ability to set surprise counter-attacks, as well as being unbelievably good at making fun of opponents by feints.' In other words, his legs seemed to have brains, too. The comparison to a chess player had not been accidental: Vienna had in fact given birth to Carl Schlechter, one of the best representatives of the discipline at international level. And Sindelar, or Motzl, played with his brain before his feet. The comparison with Schlechter was only one of many, and not even the most popular. For most, Sindelar would be the Mozart of football.

# 1

MATTHIAS SINDELAR – known in Vienna by several nicknames including Sindi, Motzl and Der Papierene, or the Paper Man – was born on 10 February 1903 in Kozlov (Kozlau in German), a small village in South Moravia near the city of Jihlava (or Iglau) whose main language was German.

Like several families from Moravia, Bohemia and Hungary, the Sindelar family – the father, Johann, was a bricklayer and the mother, Marie, was a washerwoman – moved to the imperial capital in 1905 in search of fortune. They took up residence in a suburb south of Vienna, Favoriten, along the Quellenstrasse, in a neighbourhood which had long been populated by hundreds of thousands of Bohemian and Moravian bricklayers who had emigrated to Vienna. Here, Sindelar attended the Janos Komensky school.

Since childhood, Motzl played with his peers in the streets of his neighbourhood. He and the other local children made their own way by assembling the then popular *Fetzenlaberl*, handmade footballs without any elasticity, usually consisting of multiple rags tied together. In the streets, gardens and abandoned car parks, the weak and malnourished Motzl began to develop his extraordinary talent for football.

It was in these years that the style of play characterised by agility and refinement that would later go down in history as *Scheiberlspiel* and which would enjoy wide international prominence during the 1930s, being renamed the Viennese School, began to come to life. Sindelar was not the only cheerleader, but was certainly the main one.

When Johann Sindelar died on the Isonzo in 1917, Marie found herself having to support little Matthias and the three sisters on her own. That same year, Sindelar, only 14 years old, found employment as an apprentice blacksmith. And it wasn't until the following year that Motzl's talent was noticed by Febus, an executive of Hertha Vienna, during one of the occasions when the students of the school in Favoriten were allowed to play on the local training ground, a few steps from where the Sindelar family lived. However, the theory that Sindelar's qualities had been observed even before that should not be overlooked: gardens and car parks often served as pitches for the games between boys, and besides being searched by the police, intent on banning the use of the ball in forbidden or dangerous areas, they were also monitored by the observers of the main teams of the capital.

Thus Sindelar was put under contract by Hertha Vienna, a club known to be a hotbed of future talent for the top Viennese teams. On 26 May 1918, the 15-year-old Sindelar signed his first contract.

Hertha Vienna had been founded in 1904 as Allgemeine Sport-Verein Hertha, after the break-up of another team from Favoriten, Rudolfshügel. Both Hertha and Rudolfshügel had taken part in the first official first division championship in the 1911/12 season, but came in third and second-bottom respectively. The negative trend for Hertha had continued until the end of the Great War, with the exception of fifth place at the end of the 1914/15 season.

Between 1915/16 and 1917/18, Hertha were not relegated only because during the war years the Austrian championship did not allow for promotions and relegation. In that time, the

Hertha Vienna field was used as a military base, and the club had to use the Rudolfshügel facilities. From 1917, the club had its own land, built along Quellenstrasse, the same street where the Sindelar family lived. In the following years, the stands were extended, the playing area was levelled and other structures were added, despite this needing a considerable financial outlay.

Sindelar's arrival was directly linked to the club's negative results: because of the team's unsatisfactory placings in the league, Hertha's managers had started holding trials of schoolchildren with the aim of identifying new talent. This strategy paid off and in 1920 the club came fifth, and the following year it decided to integrate some of the players from the youth line-up into the first team. Sindelar was among them, and made his debut on 8 October 1921 away at Wacker.

Rudolf Kilka, then Hertha's coach, had decided to gamble on Sindelar given the poor performance of his strikers, although Sindelar played for only 30 minutes. The match was interrupted because of an electrical storm and the remaining time was played about four months later, but on that occasion Sindelar was not selected.

That year, Sindelar played eight games without scoring. His first official goal would come the following season, on 10 September 1922 in the 2-2 draw against Admira. There is no evidence of that goal, however: the newspapers were on strike and no one reported the facts about the match.

At the beginning of the season, several strikers had left and the coach was counting on giving Sindelar and Holy, two of the club's most promising resources, more playing time. Following his first goal, the name of Matthias Sindelar had begun to echo at the Café Walloch and the Rosensäle restaurant, two of Hertha's main meeting places for fans.

Over the next two years, despite poor results, the club would remain in the first division, and in 1923 Sindelar was acclaimed by the press after a 3-2 defeat against Rapid thanks to a very fine goal.

In May of the same year, Sindelar's career suffered a worrying setback as he caused himself a serious injury – not the only one in his career – while swimming in the municipal pool in his neighbourhood. He was out for a few months, forced to look on from the sidelines. And as if that wasn't enough, he and 300 other workers were dismissed from Österreichischen Werke G.A. during that year due to the crisis. Sindelar thus returned to the pitch in the second half of the season, but without success and he ended the season without no goals as Hertha were relegated to the second division.

In the meantime, work had taken place to increase the stadium's capacity. It was now able to accommodate 30,000 people, although the numbers of previous years indicated that the turnout for matches had never exceeded 8,000. The motivation behind these investments was that the stadium would also be used to host matches and other events, but the costs would never be amortised.

Following a decline in the club's finances, Sindelar was put up for sale alongside Schneider and Reiterer. The three were sold to Wiener Amateur Sportverein for the total amount of 3,000 shillings. Although Hertha's management initially intended to sell only Sindelar for that amount, the Amateure executives, aware of the precarious finances of the Favoriten club, managed to incorporate Schneider and Reiterer into the deal. Wolfgang Hafer, grandson of Hugo Meisl, claims that behind the purchase of Matthias Sindelar was his grandfather who had already been monitoring the player for some years.

The only concerns that the Wiener management had about that purchase were of a physical nature, since Sindelar had recently suffered a serious injury and the knee problems had recurred. Emanuel Schwarz, doctor and vice-president of the club, instructed his colleague Hans Spitzy to operate on the player's knee. The operation was successful, but from that moment on Sindelar would often appear with a huge white patch on his knee, visible in several photographs of the time.

WIENER AMATEUR were going through a transitional phase and had just lost legendary striker Kalman Konrad, who together with his brother Jenő had decided to leave the club. Sindelar's official debut was on 5 October 1924 against First Vienna. On that occasion Sindelar did not score, but he had the opportunity to come up against Friedrich Gschweidl, one of the strikers with whom he would contend for the role of centre-forward with the national team during the following years. A month later, Sindelar scored his first goal with his new club against the Hakoah, after finishing a combination started by Schaffer and Neumann.

That year, however, the championship was missed by a hair's breadth and it went to Hakoah Vienna because of the defeat Amateure suffered against Wiener AC. The following year, Amateure did finish top, but Sindelar did not play a leading role in what turned out to be the only championship of his career. The player was acclaimed in the 1926/27 season, exploding and becoming the symbol of Amateure, despite the club finishing seventh and losing the final of the Vienna Cup against Rapid. On a personal level, however, Sindelar played regularly and scored 18 goals in 23 games. From then on, his favourite stage was the Vienna Cup – later renamed the Austrian Cup – and internationally the Mitropa Cup, which he would raise in 1933 and 1936.

The Mitropa Cup was the competition that most highlighted Sindelar as the strongest European player of his time. Following his 3-0 victory against Juventus in the first leg of the semi-final in 1933, *La Stampa* commented:

'The Austrians had an artist in Sindelar. Bearing in mind the result obtained by Austria, if they play the return match like today's Juventus will have big problems.'

At this time the player was nicknamed 'Der Papierene', or 'Cartavelina'. There are two different stories surrounding the source of these. The first one attributes their invention to an Austrian fan who, observing that Sindelar often lay injured on the ground, mocked his fragility. According to others, instead, they were attributed to Hugo Meisl, who often underlined Sindelar's agile and graceful style.

The opinion that Sindelar was the top player at the time was shared by journalists, team-mates and opponents. On more than one occasion he was compared to Giuseppe Meazza, his main rival for the crown of the continent's best player during the 1930s, although any preferences for one over the other were often influenced by the nationality of the writer in question. For example, the famous *La Stampa* journalist Luigi Cavallero, after the first leg of the 1933 Mitropa Cup final match won by Ambrosiana, analysed the duel between the two and wrote:

'Anyone who has waited for this match to make a comparison between the two men competing for the international best player palm will surely have been disappointed. How can you judge two players so different? Meazza is cunning, virtuous and skilful, while Sindelar is impetuous and determined ... But we can say with our eyes closed that Meazza's class exceeds Sindelar's, beyond what is said in Vienna, where the top player of Wunderteam is considered the champion par excellence.'

Another of the attackers who dominated those years was the Belgian Raymond Braine, star of Sparta Prague. Sindelar and Braine would face each other on more than one occasion in the Mitropa Cup. *Sport-Tagblatt* drew a comparison between the two before the 1936 Mitropa Cup final, 'Sindelar and Braine are two great leaders. The Belgian plays at a slow pace, while Sindelar is a more agile and creative player. Braine is a more reliable finisher, while Sindelar shoots more at goal by virtue of momentary inspirations, which makes him even more dangerous.'

Ernst Reitermaier, a former Wacker Wien striker, once said of Sindelar, 'When he wanted to move to the left, he faked to the right. He was always doing the opposite of what the opponent expected.' Otto Fodrek, another Wacker Wien legend, simply described Sindelar with one word, 'phenomena'. After a 4-0 victory in a friendly played at the Parc des Princes against France, home forward Paul Nicolas said that among all the members of the Wunderteam the one who impressed him the most was Sindelar, because of his ability to link with his team-mates but at the same time to influence the game thanks to his individual virtues.

Sindelar had become the centre-forward and symbol of FK Austria – a name that Die Veilchen would take on from 1926 – a society traditionally associated with the liberal Jewish bourgeoisie, a frequenter of Bohemian life and the coffee houses of the metropolis. Over the years, there were several clubs who, being aware of the precarious finances of FK Austria, a situation common to several teams in the inter-war period, tried to snatch Sindelar from FK Austria. They were approached by Rapid, willing to pay a sum of 35m crowns. From England, Arsenal put £40,000 forward, and Charlton Athletic, through the English manager Jimmy Seed, were also interested. Finally Slavia Prague tried to replace the legendary forward František Svoboda with Sindelar. But Motzl had refused every offer, and over the years he would become an icon of Austria Vienna and one of the most popular players – if not the most popular – in the history of the club.

His career with his club ended on 11 December 1938 when he played his last official match in the purple-and-white shirt, although Sindelar would make his final appearance against Hertha Berlin on Boxing Day. From that moment on, the young forward Johann Safarik would regularly appear in Sindelar's place, and FK Austria were renamed FK Ostmark Wien for a few months. Austrian football had returned to amateurism, as had been the will of the Reich which renamed the Austrian championship the Gauliga Ostmark, a regional tournament at the end of which the winner would take part in the German championship. In addition, the Nazis had forced the Jewish leaders of Austria to leave their jobs. The first to pay the price was president Emanuel Schwarz, with whom Sindelar had always maintained a relationship of mutual respect, almost friendship. In a letter he wrote to the player:

'The new Führer of Austria Vienna has forbidden us to greet you, but I will always want to say "Good morning" to you whenever I am lucky enough to meet you.'

One amusing anecdote saw Sindelar approach Schwarz and ask him for an advance on part of his salary to pay some important expenses. Schwarz asked him how much, and Sindelar answered smilingly, 'Twenty shillings.'

## 3

SINDELAR WAS not the only pillar of the Wunderteam whose talent had sprouted in the infamous suburbs of the capital. Several members of the future Austrian team had a similar story behind them: as children they had had to make do by playing in the lanes and in the streets using lamps as posts and balls tied up with anything they could find.

This provoked regular conflict with the police, the parking lot attendants and anyone involved in the surveillance of public spaces. The disrespect and dislike for the authorities, together with the feeling of always having to fight for something, was probably the basis of the style of play that would distinguish Viennese football in the years to come, the trademark known as the 'Viennese School'.

The first idol of the Viennese crowds was Josef 'Pepi' Uridil, nicknamed 'The Tank', a boy who, like Matthias Sindelar, was the son of economic migrants who moved to the Viennese suburbs and soon became an icon of SK Rapid. Sindelar's fame, however, would go far beyond that of Uridil: he became the Wunderteam artist, the player who more than anyone else would embody its style of play.

No one would have represented the art of Viennese football of the time better than he did, characterised by sophisticated technique, intelligent movements and precise ground passages. According to chroniclers of the time, Sindelar 'read the game as the actors interpreted their scripts, directed his team as the greatest composers of classical music conducted their orchestras and wrote drafts and stories on the field just as literary celebrities did in Vienna's coffee houses'.

Sindelar's Austria debut was on 28 September 1926 against Czechoslovakia, in which he scored. Between 1928 and 1931, however, Sindelar was called only once. After a quarrel with Hugo Meisl at the end of a resounding friendly defeat to Germany, the coach, displeased by the player's attitude, decided to leave him out. In reality, Sindelar had not been the only one to be dropped: First Vienna forward Fritz Gschweidl was too. In spite of this, they both returned to occupy the centre of the Wunderteam attack in the early 1930s, when Meisl went back to Vienna following an illness that had kept him away from the national team's bench.

In any case, Meisl continued to show some hesitation and on more than one occasion he had decided to do without Austria Vienna's centre-forward. After a few omissions, Sindelar returned to the heart of the attack on a special occasion: the friendly played at the Hohe Warte Stadium in Vienna against Scotland on 16 May 1931, which ended 5-0 to the Austrians. On that occasion, Sindelar scored the fifth goal and gave a stellar performance. That was the occasion when Austria became the Wunderteam for everyone, and Sindelar was the main protagonist.

In the following 11 matches the Wunderteam remained unbeaten, winning on nine occasions and drawing twice in a positive streak that lasted for a year and a half. In articles in the Austrian newspapers, the discussions inevitably focused on the teamwork shown by Meisl's men and, on an individual level, on the feints, the unpredictable style and changes of direction highlighted by the Wunderteam star that no opposing defender seemed to be able to predict and anticipate.

Sindelar – who after that performance had definitely moved up in his coach's estimation – had led his team to a series of extraordinary successes.

His fame grew as well outside the playing field and like Uridil before him, Sindelar became a true icon. He was chosen as an advocate for wristwatches and dairy products and also starred in a film based on an article, entitled *Roxy und das Wunderteam*. And just like Uridil, he hadn't become big-headed. He had remained true to his profession and his city.

His contribution was crucial in winning the 1931/32 International Cup: he scored four goals and was the team's second goalscorer after Anton Schall, but having played only five games, all since his feat against Scotland.

While the International Cup was under way, Austria played a friendly against Hungary on 24 April 1932 and won 8-2 on a day that went down in history as being Sindelar's best performance: he scored his second hat-trick for the national team and received plenty of praise. Hungarian coach Lajos Máriássy, for example, claimed that Sindelar was a player 'of a higher class'. In *Kicker* magazine, former Amateure player and manager Johann Leute wrote, 'Sindelar proved to be a centre-forward with vision unimaginable to any football fan.' *Reichpost* wrote that 60,000 people had applauded 'that blond centre-forward at the expense of the election rallies', as municipal elections were being held that day in Austria. Leute added, 'We usually think of an English player as the prototype of the footballer, but after what we saw on the pitch on Sunday we can say that we have our best Austrian version at home.'

Sindelar's international peak coincided with his participation in the 1934 World Cup, to which Austria went as one of the favourites for the title. The competition, however, didn't produce the satisfaction that Matthias and his companions would have hoped for.

However, his performance was very positive: in the round of 16 against France he scored the equalising goal after a solo breakaway and then watched Schall and Bican score the other two, while in the quarter-finals he was chosen as the team's star player by the local newspaper *Il Tifone*. In the semi-final defeat to Italy he was a key focal point for his team-mates, who on more than one occasion did not take advantage of his passes. After the competition, Sindelar stayed in Milan to assess the condition of his knee. In the meantime, the other members of the Wunderteam had returned to Vienna in a hurry, partly to forget their disappointment and partly because the football season was still going on. After a few days the Mitropa Cup started, with the players from Admira, FK Austria and Rapid fighting for the title against their historical rivals.

From that moment on, Sindelar's international appearances gradually decreased. Meisl had decided to replace him with Josef Bican, partly because of Sindelar's repeated knee injuries and partly to refresh the team. Other attackers had also been included, albeit less frequently, such as Binder, Donnenfeld, Walzhofer and Durspekt.

Sindelar's last appearance in the International Cup was a 3-1 defeat against Hungary in Budapest. On that occasion, he had a goal disallowed for offside, wrongly in the opinion of many observers.

The 4-4 draw against Hungary on 6 October marked a transition as Josef Bican scored a hat-trick and consolidated his place in the centre of the attack. Sindelar, due to an injury, didn't even take part in the match.

Then the Anschluss took over, and with it came the end of the Wunderteam and its dreams of glory. In 1938, after having already practically hung up their boots, Austria played the *Anschlussspiel*, the 'connection match' against German on 3 April. Sindelar scored, Austria won 2-0 and Germany coach

Sepp Herberger began to call some Wunderteam players to the training sessions held in Germany to select the nation's players for the 1938 World Cup. Sindelar, however, would always reject this opportunity by citing repeated knee discomfort.

## 4

SINDELAR HAD never supported any political party in public, although some claimed that in private he made no secret of his social democratic inclinations. He was loved as much in 'Red Vienna' as in the Catholic, monarchist and reactionary suburbs. The crisis was raging in Vienna but in the world of football the Austrian capital had maintained its reputation as a pioneering city. And Sindelar had played an important role.

On a personal level, all the accounts and testimonies of the time seem to indicate that Sindelar was shy and a man of few words. He was not a drinker but was often caught smoking, even during the national team retreats despite the prohibitions imposed by his coach. As Camilo Francka reported in his book *Matthias Sindelar: Una Historia de Fútbol, Nazismo y Misterios*, Nortbert Lopper, a former manager of Austria, once recounted, 'During a game against the Hakoah in 1937, Sindelar was sitting in the press box and I was lucky enough to find myself in the line in front of him. We had a chat. I still remember his tone of voice, it was greatly influenced by the fact that he smoked a lot.'

Sindelar did not like to have the spotlight on him. The more he stayed away from microphones and journalists, the happier he was. On 7 July 1932, the Wunderteam were invited to Stockholm for a friendly. Before the match began, King Gustav V of Sweden asked Sindelar if he was comfortable in Stockholm. After a few seconds of embarrassment, he timidly replied that he was. The monarch also asked him to make a public speech. His companions asked him at the end of that speech if he felt honoured by that request and Sindelar replied, 'Yes, but one should not be forced to give a speech.'

Following the Anschluss, Austrian players had to look for paid employment because the transition to amateur football prevented clubs from paying out wages. Sindelar bought the Annahof, a coffee house at the intersection of Laxemburgerstrasse and Dampfgasse, in the district where he grew up, Favoriten. His knee called for a truce, and Austrian football, which had regressed by 15 years, no longer motivated him.

This choice was, however, symptomatic of the fact that Sindelar had decided not to leave Vienna, despite the German invasion and pressure to join the national team trained by Sepp Herberger. And it wasn't only through the purchase of the Annahof that Sindelar, after the end of his playing career, had taken economic precautions: he had become manager of Pohl, a local sports goods company that produced, among other things, the WIPO-Sindelar soccer ball, and had also bought a grocery store.

Among other things, in March 1938 Sindelar was appointed by Thomas Kozich, one of the deputy mayors of Vienna, as director of the company in charge of the renovation of the Prater (a large public park in Vienna), a position for which the player showed great pride and contentment. Life went on, despite the fact that his career as a footballer was behind him and Austria had become a fully-fledged German colony.

# 5

ON THE morning of 23 January 1939, Sindelar was found dead together with his partner, Camilla Castagnola, a girl he had been seeing for some weeks. The bodies were found in Castagnola's apartment in Annagasse. The days following the event were full of all kinds of rumours about what happened: some spoke of suicide and others of murder, although the Innere Stadt police of the first district of Vienna claimed that the main cause of death had been a gas leak. The Gestapo investigators had arrived in no time, probably because of the notoriety of the victims, and had questioned the neighbours, several of whom had pointed out how the stove had been emitting smoke and gas for days. Egon Ulbrich, manager of FK Austria and a close friend of Sindelar, reconstructed the events of the previous night, 'We had arranged an evening with several friends at Café Weidinger. We played cards all night and had a lot of money up for grabs. I think some friends wanted to make fun of *Sindi*, maybe even trick him. We played and drank all night.'

Sindelar then headed towards an apartment along the Annagasse, where Camilla, his new companion, lived.

On Camilla – as well as on Sindelar – various unfounded rumours have circulated over the years. According to some, Camilla was an Italian-Jewish immigrant who had been a supporter of the Fascist Party until 1938. Sindelar had met her years before, at the end of the 1934 World Cup at a hospital where she was working. According to this version, the two moved together to Vienna, where Camilla changed jobs and became an Italian teacher. From 1938, however, the problems began: because of her religion, Camilla had to leave her job.

Another theory, based in part on the fact that Sindelar had only engaged in impromptu, short-term romantic relationships over the years, claimed that Castagnola was a prostitute.

However, more reliable sources indicate that Camilla was Austrian, born in Vienna as Camilla Durspect, and that she acquired the Italian surname only after her marriage to an Italian immigrant, Mario Castagnola. She had been a nurse, but when Sindelar met her, Camilla owned the restaurant Zum Weißen Rössel. After her death, she was buried at the cemetery in Ottakring. In any case, few testimonies remain: someone had stressed her nervous and possessive character, claiming that on more than one occasion she had called Sindelar and urged him to come to her restaurant.

There were several rumours among the Viennese population about the death of the couple: for some, Sindelar had committed suicide; for others he had been killed. According to the latter, the leaders of the Third Reich would not have reacted well to his alleged failure to say goodbye at the end of the *Anschlussspiel* and his subsequent refusal to represent the German national team at the World Cup. Two of the most important intellectuals of the time, Friedrich Torberg and Alfred Polgar, espoused the thesis of suicide, but not for the reasons mentioned above. In his famous *Ballad on the Death of a Footballer*, Friedrich Torberg argued that Sindelar had taken his own life so that he would no longer have to live in the barbarity that reigned over Austrian football. Alfred Polgar expressed himself along the same lines, 'The good Sindelar did not detach himself from that city of which he was the son and pride until his death. Everything leads us to think of a death caused by his loyalty to his country. To live and play football in such a tormented, destroyed and oppressed city would have meant betraying it. How could you play under such conditions? Or to live, when a life without football is nothing?'

Another of the unfounded theories was that the player had been killed because of his religion. Some wrote that Sindelar was Jewish, others that he was of Jewish origin and that the Gestapo was investigating his lineage. An investigation began but did not have a definitive and official outcome. Several books and articles over the years put these ideas into circulation, passing them off as certain. The credibility enjoyed by these hypotheses was probably due to the unbreakable bond between the player and his club, FK Austria, given its strong Jewish characterisation. Moreover, such a narrative lent itself perfectly to a romantic and rebellious image of a champion whose heroic deeds had instead remained confined to the playing field.

As noted, Sindelar was born in a village of the then Protectorate of Moravia in which the Jewish presence over the centuries had drastically decreased to the point of almost zero. Between 1627 and 1628, the Revised Constitution came into force in Bohemia and Moravia, which through one of its articles indicated the Catholic religion as the only one recognised by the state. This had significantly reduced the freedoms of Protestants and Jews, who had emigrated to other shores. Although Emperor Joseph II in 1781 abolished discriminatory laws to the detriment of Jews – which is why the Jewish quarter of the capital, Prague, was to be renamed Josefov – the Jewish presence in Moravia had not recovered, as demonstrated by the fact that it accounted for only 2.2 per cent of the total population around the middle of the 20th century. It was a minimum percentage that did not include the Sindelar family. Sindelar, in fact, is not a Jewish surname, and all official documents relating to the player or his family are unequivocal: Sindelar was Catholic.

'Der Papierene' was not the only player whose roots would be misinterpreted: two other players belonging to the Wunderteam, Camillo Jerusalem and Karl Zischek, were also said to be Jewish, although there is no official source to corroborate this. Between 1931 and 1938 no Jewish players had been part of the Wunderteam: Hugo Meisl had called some Jewish players to the ranks but this had happened in the 1920s and always for the benefit of players of Hakoah Vienna, in the years when Hakoah had been one of the most important teams in the capital. The likes of Katz, Häusler, Scheuer, Grünwald, Fried, Neufeld – aka Nemes – and Wortmann all featured.

Among the many myths proliferating was also that the National Socialist regime had denied the autopsy. In fact, the autopsy, conducted by Dr Schneider of the Institute of Forensic Medicine of the University of Vienna, took place on 26 January, and confirmed as the cause of death a carbon monoxide inhalation intoxication with a consequent reduction of blood. One of the hypotheses that had been taken into consideration, namely poisoning, was definitely discarded.

The death of the player at the will of the Reich was just one of the many myths that surrounded Matthias Sindelar. He became a hero and icon of resistance without his knowledge, and without his ever having wanted it. He was a great player, not the hero who would be painted in the decades following his death.

## 6

WHEN SINDELAR bought the Café Annahof on 15 June 1938, he took it over from a Jewish citizen, Leopold Drill, whose business had been Aryanised. Drill was forced to sell his business for much less than its real value. Sindelar, after having sworn to be of Aryan descent, paid 15,000 marks in cash and the remaining 5,000 in six-monthly instalments of 300 in addition to the Aryanisation tax imposed by the National Socialist regime for a total value much lower than the one estimated by Drill, which was around 54,000 marks.

Sindelar, therefore, benefited from the situation as did several Viennese citizens of the time. Karl Sesta, the other alleged hero of the *Anschlussspiel* and close friend of Sindelar, also took advantage of a similar scenario: he obtained a licence to run one of the coffee houses and bakeries belonging to the Hammerbröt-werke franchisor, whose previous owner, Josef Brand, was Jewish. So did former First Vienna defender Karl Rainer, who received an Aryanised apartment for a favourable price. Drill was later deported to Theresienstadt and died in an extermination camp in 1943.

Sindelar, let it be clear, was not a Nazi: over the years he had become the star of a team representing the Viennese Jewish bourgeoisie and had always maintained excellent relations with the Jewish leadership of his club, first of all

Emanuel Schwarz. However, an opportunity had presented itself and he had not hesitated to grasp it.

Following his death, the Café Sindelar, the former Annahof, was confiscated. His sisters – two of them, since the third had died years earlier – had no way of taking over the business. They were informed by the head of the Viennese section of the NSDAP (National Socialist German Workers' Party) that the decision to confiscate the premises was based on the 'pro-Jewish views expressed by the brother together with his negative attitude towards the party'. However, regardless of the events at the Annahof, Sindelar had sniffed out a business opportunity and seized it. The Annahof was supposed to represent his future away from the playing fields: to buy it, the former player even went into debt with the Gösser brewery, which in return demanded to be able to display its products inside the premises.

Sindelar, since the purchase of the business, had taken a decidedly diplomatic stance: he had invited several party leaders to the opening of his cafeteria, and in an interview he said he was 'confident about the future of Austrian football', claiming that malnourished children in previous years had returned to feeding properly.

Following his death, the National Socialists called Sindelar 'the best soldier in Viennese football' and organised a state funeral in his honour, which was later revoked the following year because these manifestations of grief were not 'in line with the times', as they disrespected the deaths that occurred day after day on the battlefields.

Despite this, Matthias Sindelar was remembered everywhere. In the coffee houses, he was described as an artist capable of embodying the main characteristics of Vienna at the time: lightness, grace, sense of humour and unbridled genius. His former club dedicated the south stand of its stadium to him, and his city named a street, Sindelargasse, after him.

In the autumn of 1973, FK Austria had also thought of naming its stadium after him, but the death of Franz Horr, former president of the Vienna Football Association, had led the club's management to opt for a different choice. Both in Kozlov, the city where he was born, and in front of the apartment where he died, two commemorative plaques appeared.

It was probably his ability to elevate football to art, together with the international limelight that had seen him as the star for club and country, that allowed Sindelar to imprint in the memories of the Viennese public a more indelible tale than those who had preceded him.

In the national imagination, Matthias Sindelar had become the hero who better than anyone else represented the poor and orphaned boy who, thanks to his talent and his efforts, had managed to triumph against adversity. The street boy who came from the Ziegelböhmen circles and who had never denied his origins, despite the fact that over the years he had begun to be revered even in bourgeois coffee houses. As Torberg once said, 'Sindelar was loved by every Viennese who knew him, in other words he was loved by everyone.'

# VII

# THE 1934 WORLD CUP IN MUSSOLINI'S ITALY

*The Wunderteam made it to their first World Cup as big favourites, despite the fact that the ÖFB had asked to postpone the event until 1936 because of financial problems, which were not only affecting the Austrian federation. In addition to the reputation that surrounded the Wunderteam, the popularity of Austrian football was also due to other factors: Austria Vienna triumphed in the most recent edition of the Mitropa Cup thanks to the victory in the two-legged final against Giuseppe Meazza's Ambrosiana, and when the World Cup began, the third edition of the International Cup was still in progress and saw Italy leading the standings with six points, two more than Austria, who had, however, won the direct confrontation 4-2. The Wunderteam, however, had played three games fewer and had an excellent chance of overtaking Pozzo's men. Benito Mussolini's Italy hosted the World Cup after the first edition had been held in Uruguay and had not been entered by most famous European teams, partly because of the high travel costs and partly because of the protest against the failure of Jules Rimet and the FIFA summits to host the first edition in Europe. Hugo Meisl, for example, disagreed with this decision: although he had helped to create the World Cup, he would have preferred South American teams to adapt due to the greater prevalence of European contenders.*

# 1

IN 1930, when the first World Cup took place, the FIFA leadership had chosen Uruguay as the host nation. Uruguay was celebrating the 100th anniversary of its constitution which, among other things, had decreed the abolition of slavery and the expulsion of the military from parliament.

Uruguay's democratic identity was so strong that year that within a week, from 11 to 18 July, three events were celebrated: the anniversary of the flag, the Taking of the Bastille – an event not directly linked to local history – and, indeed, the 100th anniversary of the constitution. In order to have a clear idea of how much Uruguay was a country in the vanguard of democratic battles, one must remember that the neighbouring countries of Argentina and Brazil abolished slavery in 1888 and 1853 respectively. Moreover, Uruguay was the only South American nation to have in previous years deployed mulatto – people of mixed black African and white European ancestry – players in the South American Campeonato, the forerunner of today's Copa America, including the attackers Juan Delgado and Isabelo Gradin. Chile had complained on one occasion about the presence of the two 'Africans' on the pitch. Also, in the first edition of the World Cup – as well as in the two Olympic events that preceded it – Uruguay had highlighted José Leandro Andrade, who was the son of African slaves and was considered to be one of the greatest players of his time. On the occasion of the 100th anniversary of the constitution, the El Centenario stadium was inaugurated in Montevideo with a capacity of 80,000 spectators, enormous for those times, especially for a city still moderately populated. It did, however, demonstrate the passion for football that the Charrua people had cultivated in previous decades. This was reflected in the already bitter rivalry between Peñarol and Nacional, the two clubs who competed for the title and the honour of being the best team in the capital.

That climate of openness and tolerance was the reason why the FIFA summits had accepted Uruguay as hosts. In a Europe that was being undermined by authoritarianism and totalitarianism, the political pressure on such a globally publicised event would have been much greater.

However, following the meeting of 8 October 1932, the FIFA Assembly decided to entrust the organisation of the second edition of the World Cup to the FIGC, the Italian Football Federation. The main reason would have been the possibility of hosting the various matches in eight stadiums with sufficient capacity, which would have eliminated one of the main criticisms of the 1930 event, namely a reduced number of venues capable of holding tens of thousands of spectators. The PNF Stadium – National Fascist Party – in Rome could hold 45,000, even though it was initially designed for 30,000. The architect, inspired by the Hellenic tradition, had been able to make a change: he had joined the two horseshoe-shaped grandstands in a transversal row. Then there was the San Siro in Milan, used only for football competitions, which on special occasions could seat 50,000 people, while the Mussolini in Turin could seat as many as 70,000. There were also the Berta Stadium in Florence (45,000), the Municipal Stadium in Naples (45,000), the Littoriale Stadium in Bologna (50,000), the recently renovated

Luigi Ferraris Stadium in Genoa (51,000) and finally the Littorio in Trieste (25,000).

Secondly, it should also be pointed out that in those years the possibility of the Second World War seemed to be far off: Hitler had only been settled for a year, and relations between him and Mussolini had frozen when Austrian Chancellor Engelbert Dollfuss was assassinated.

Mussolini had attributed that attack directly to Adolf Hitler and had deployed his troops at the Brenner border in order to keep a possible German advance under control.

Also, a clearly xenophobic outlook did not yet exist in Muslim rhetoric and fascist politics. Proof of this was the fact that Mussolini himself had pushed for the inclusion in Vittorio Pozzo's national team of players such as Luis Monti, nicknamed the 'Colossus', the first scorer in the history of Argentina at the World Cup and a finalist in 1930, plus Enrique Guaita and Raimundo 'Mumo' Orsi.

In Mussolini's Italy, the foreigner par excellence was the Austrian, a clear legacy of the Great War. And Italy fought that war not only with Austria but also with Hungary and Czechoslovakia, three nations whose army had threatened its borders only a few years before. A defeat would not have been well received.

## 2

THE FORMAT was substantially different from that of 1930. The number of participants – 13 in 1930 – had risen to 16, who had to compete in qualifying rounds to reach the finals. The Wunderteam were placed in Group 4 together with Hungary and Bulgaria. They beat Bulgaria 6-1 thanks to Horvath's hat-trick and goals from Zischeck, Viertl and Sindelar. They qualified as Bulgaria, who had also lost to Hungary, could no longer qualify and withdrew.

Austria and Hungary qualified for the finals, where the competition changed format with direct knockout rounds beginning with the last 16.

The days before the start of the competition were marked by analysis and discussions about the favourites. Jules Rimet said, 'My big favourite is Italy. In addition to the desire to prevail over others, they will also have the motivation to overcome themselves and serve their country in each of the acts of the competition … I put the Austrian national team just behind Italy. The virtues of the Austrians have no equal throughout the continent.'

That opinion was echoed by Argentine striker Manuel Nolo Ferreira, who felt that Austria would be the number one danger for the home team. Among the favourites were Hungary, including rising star and future captain Gyorgy Sarosi who, being half-Italian, spoke the language fluently and coached several clubs in the country later in his career. Also among the Hungarian ranks were Újpest duo László Sternberg and Istvan Avar: the former was defender and captain, while the latter was a formidable goal machine. Újpest had won the previous edition of the Hungarian championship and would also triumph in the first one after the World Cup. Another player of international fame was Istvan Palotas, the MTK striker who many pointed out was the Hungarian pioneer of the role of a false nine, even before Nandor Hidegkuti, by virtue of his ability to break away from his position as a striker and act as a creator for the other members of the attacking line.

Another of the main contenders were Czechoslovakia, who counted talents such as the gunner Oldřich 'Olda' Nejedlý. Nejedlý would be the leading scorer in the competition and with his club team, Sparta Prague, was part of one of the strongest attacks in Europe together with the Belgian Raymond Braine. Then there was the legendary goalkeeper František Plánička and striker Antonín Puč, who would become the greatest goalscorer of all time for the Czechoslovak national team.

As far as the South American teams were concerned, given the absence of the defending champions Uruguay and an Argentina not as good as four years before, the favourites were Brazil. The Uruguayans had declined the invitation because of Italy's lack of participation in the previous edition, adding that they were against the 'fascist regime and the political use that would be made of the event'. Brazil, for their part, trained by coach Luiz Vinhaes, could boast among their ranks Leônidas da Silva, famous for having helped to perfect the famous bicycle kick. In Brazil, Leônidas is mistakenly named as the instigator of this technique gesture, although the first to perform it was a Chilean, Ramón Unzaga.

Among the favourites were Italy, and not only because they were the hosts. Important names stood out among the *Azzurri*: first of all that of Giuseppe Meazza, defeated in the final of the last Mitropa Cup by Austria Vienna. Meazza preferred to act as an attacker, but his incredible repertoire allowed him to play in a deeper role as well, thanks to his ability to send his team-mates through on goal. As centre-forward he would have played with Angelo Schiavio, with Borel on the bench ready to take over if more speed was required. In goal was Gianpiero Combi, considered one of the best goalkeepers in the world with Zamora and Plánička. Others among the most talented players were Guaita, Orsi and Monti, at his second World Cup, but the first with the Italian squad.

And finally were the other big favourites, Austria, who were accepted as playing a unique and avant-garde brand of football. The Italian concerns were largely justified by what had happened in the previous edition of the Mitropa Cup, when FK Austria had got the better of Ambrosiana and won the trophy. Moreover, Austria raised the International Cup two years earlier.

Hugo Meisl, who had resumed coaching the Austrian national team after the end of the Great War, had never considered changing his formation, the pyramid, as it is still defined today.

But despite this, Meisl seemed worried: he wanted Jimmy Hogan at his side once again as a collaborator, but due to the limited finances available to the ÖFB this was not possible and Meisl had to make do with Franz Hansl, a former player from Austria Vienna who at least had an excellent knowledge of Italian football having coached Torino, Alessandria, Livorno and Salernitana.

# 3

MEISL ONLY called up 16 players to his squad. There were surprising exclusions, such as those of two of the rising stars of Austrian football, the forwards Franz Binder and Rudolf Hahnemann, as well as the injury-enforced absence of Walter Nausch, who remained in Vienna. The coach had decided to join Matthias Sindelar with the exceptional talent of Josef Bican, the prolific goalscoring of Admira's Anton Schall, the speed of SC Wacker Wien's Karl Zischek and the experience of forward Rudolf Viertl, who perfectly understood Sindelar as the two were team-mates at FK Austria.

Meisl, on the other hand, had fewer doubts about the other areas of the team. In goal was Peter Platzer of FC Admira Wacker Mödling; in defence were Karl Sesta, who was to join Sindelar and Viertl at Austria Vienna, and Franz Cisar of Wiener AC. The midfield trio, which would never change during the competition, consisted of Wagner, Smistik and Urbanek, the first two from Rapid and the third from Admira.

The Wunderteam arrived in Italy by train after leaving the country's largest station, Südbanhof. The compartments were equipped with beds and the players travelled in pairs. Sindelar, for example, shared the journey with Viertl. They arrived in Italy on 22 May and decided to stay at the Hotel Dock in the centre of Turin. Curiously, both Sindelar and Sesta arrived with a toothache. For Sindelar it was a minor problem, while Sesta still had pain in the following days.

In order to accustom players to the Italian heat, Meisl decided to hold training sessions at noon, the hottest time of the day. The day before their opening game, the players competed in two speed races. Meisl had put six fountain pens up for grabs for the first arrivals. Josef Bican came first on both occasions, and Meisl, who was well aware of his striker's competitiveness, said, 'When there is something up for grabs, it could be anything.' The training sessions were usually held by Hansl, with Meisl just giving some advice. He ordered Karl Zischek to cut his hair, for example, as he said the lock of his hair could obstruct his view during the matches.

Meisl had also spoken about Matthias Sindelar:

'Sindelar is in excellent shape. On Sunday, if he is well, he will surprise the public in Turin. They say I got in his way. Nothing could be more false. I excluded him from the team when it didn't work, and now that he's in good shape I've summoned him again. It's a shame that he's over 31, because few aces like him are born, even in Austria. The exclusion from a few matches helped him. Now he's showing more desire.'

The round of 16 matches were all held on the same day, 27 May, one at each of the stadiums chosen to host the competition. The Wunderteam played France at the Mussolini Stadium in Turin, the same venue where just a few months previously they had defeated Italy.

Against France, the Wunderteam found it more difficult than they expected. The French started strong, surprising the Austrians at the start, and in the first minute Platzer had to intervene. Shortly afterwards, he found himself in front of Nicolas, and instead of shooting, fell to the ground: he seemed to faint, probably because of the torrid climate that reigned over Turin. Nicolas left the field but he was soon able to continue and in the 18th minute that choice paid off when he scored the opening goal of the game. From then onwards, Austria took control while Nicolas's precarious condition saw him continue to feel sick and his performance was affected. Austria went on the attack and twice hit the post within the space of just a few seconds, through Schall and Bican, and on the counter-attack Keller almost doubled France's lead. Then, after an anonymous performance so far, Matthias Sindelar took advantage of a mistake by French defender Mattler to equalise.

The 90 minutes ended in a draw after a boring second half in which the fear of losing losing both teams, and only in extra time did the Austrians' talent emerge thanks to goals from Schall and Bican who sealed the passage to the quarter-finals. Schall's goal was contested for a few minutes by the French players, claiming offside, and the French themselves scored a penalty four minutes from the end.

Meanwhile, the list of title contenders had shortened as Italy, Spain, Hungary, Czechoslovakia, Switzerland, Germany, Sweden and Austria had moved on to the next phase. There was a big surprise as Leônidas's Brazil, defeated by Spain, had been knocked out. Leônidas had managed to beat the normally invincible goalkeeper Zamora, but the result had already been pretty much wrapped up by two goals from Iraragorri and one from Langara between the 18th and 29th minutes. There had been another surprise, although not as big as Spain beating Brazil, as Sweden put out Argentina, the beaten finalists just four years previously.

In the quarter-finals, Austria and Hungary played the Danube derby at the Littoriale Stadium in Bologna. In the round of 16, as predicted, Hungary had got rid of Egypt with a 4-2 win, thus avenging their defeat from ten years earlier in the Olympic Games in Paris. The two Danube teams were very similar. Both pushed for victory throughout the game and both were imbued with the Scottish philosophy of the passing game.

Austria and Hungary were perhaps the two best-known teams in that World Cup. They had played the first international match between continental sides in 1902 and by 1897 their respective club teams had already competed first in the Challenge Cup and then in the Mitropa Cup, starting in 1927. And from that same year the two national teams also competed in the International Cup. Pre-match predictions were in favour of the Austrians, who won 5-2 in a friendly played in Vienna on 15 April of that year.

Jules Rimet previewed the tie with a simple message, 'A gift for lovers of the beautiful game.' He claimed to have seen a 'motivated and aggressive' Hungary and a 'smarter and more scientific' Austria. Hugo Meisl, on the other hand, was of a different opinion: although satisfied with the first half, he was disappointed by the second half.

After beating France, Meisl made just one change – replacing the injured Schall with Horvath. Hungary introduced prolific Újpest forward Istvan Avar, top scorer four years earlier in the Coupe de Nations in Geneva, and the promising youngster Gyorgy Sarosi. Making room were Pál Teleki and Gabor Szabo.

After only five minutes the seemingly brave choice to replace Schall with Horvath had already paid off as the 31-year-old forward – captain for the occasion – scored first with a good shot after an exchange between Sindelar and Bican. There followed a first half in which neither team hid. Austria continued in search of a second goal but the half-time whistle of the Italian referee Mattea kept the score at 1-0.

A few minutes into the second half, Zischek made the score 2-0 from a precise Bican assist. There was a puff of the cheeks for Meisl, who began to feel that a quarter-final place was on the way. The match, however, took a turn that Meisl didn't like at all: Bican made a bad intervention on Toldi, picking up an injury, and shortly afterwards the Hungarian captain Sternberg knocked out Horvath. In the 61st minute, a penalty converted by Sarosi raised doubts about Austria's chances but a couple of minutes later the Hungarian forward Imre Markos was sent off. The tie remained at 2-1 until its conclusion.

At the time, there was an ongoing debate over which of the two central European teams was better. It was a discussion as old as the birth of football in both countries. That day Austria's victory gave a fairly clear answer: the Wunderteam had something extra, and that victory was confirmation of the superiority shown in the previous edition of the International Cup. The pre-match predictions had not been disregarded.

Four teams were left to compete for the World Cup: Austria, Italy, Czechoslovakia and Germany, after a set of quarter-finals with no surprises. Austria would face the hosts in the semi-final as Italy had got the better of Spain after a replay on 1 June. The first match ended 1-1 and the following day the Italians won 1-0. Over the years there was speculation about the mysterious absences from the Spain side of Zamora and the Basque attacking duo Iraragorri and Langara, who did not seem to have suffered any injuries in the first match. Some argued that these exclusions were due to pressure from the fascist regime. Zamora was allegedly caught watching the match sitting next to Hugo Meisl, who was present at the stadium as an interested spectator.

Italy v Austria wasn't just any game. If Austria v Hungary had been a match between former comrades at the front, Italy v Austria was the exact opposite. The memories of the battles of the Isonzo, Caporetto and those fought on the Piave were still raw. The players of both sides knew it well, especially the two top stars, Giuseppe Meazza and Matthias Sindelar. The two, both war orphans, had become friends over the years. But on this occasion that would have counted for nothing: it was even said that Vittorio Pozzo had shown up inside the Italian dressing room with a gramophone, and that the players had been singing 'Canzone del Piave' at the top of their lungs. For Benito Mussolini, to lose against the enemy, 'the foreigner', just could not be contemplated. The foreigner, as the 'Canzone del Piave' said, could not pass, despite the fact that in 1934 diplomatic relations between the two countries were more than solid.

Regardless of the political scenario, Italy–Austria was for many an early final and for this reason there were plenty of people who believed that the San Siro was inadequate to host the event due to its limited capacity. Some would have preferred Turin's Mussolini Stadium, with more seats and therefore better suited to hold Italian fans flocking from all corners of the kingdom. The turnout was a record 40,000 spectators, which meant it was sold out. According to some, the crowd inside the ground exceeded that number and reached 45,000.

Carlo Roghi, journalist for *La Gazzetta dello Sport*, said of the Italian national team:

'They, in so many years of sporting fights with the Austrians, managed to beat them twice: once in Milan, and it was an exciting match, and once in Trieste. Today Italy had greater chances of winning. There are new men in the wards, the atmosphere of the match has changed. Moreover, the cup has its own laws that cannot be deciphered. Austrians and Italians can, without ostentation or arrogance, pretend to have in their hands the good weapons to win.'

Mussolini was present in the stands, and Jules Rimet, as per protocol, had sat to his right. Not far away, Rimet had also met again with several members of the royal family, as he had done prior to Italy's first game, against the USA: the Prince of Savoy, the Prince of Piedmont, the Duke of Spoleto, Princess Mafalda, Princess Maria di Savoia and other ministers. All of them seemed to be willing to exchange a few impressions about the game apart from the Duke. Mussolini, in fact, followed the matches with extreme concentration, without ever uttering a word. Rimet said that he never had the opportunity to speak with Mussolini, unlike four years earlier when the Uruguayan president Juan Campisteguy had invited him to taste what was an absolute novelty for Rimet: the asado, the South American barbecue. Rimet quickly realised that Campisteguy was more interested in his origins than in his institutional figure, since the Uruguayan president himself had transalpine origins.

Before the match, Milan had been the victim of a storm and at kick-off the pitch was still soaked, leading to concerns that it would impact the quality of football on show. This could have benefited those who, on paper, had less technique – Pozzo's Italy. Meisl, who wasn't happy with his team in the quarter-final against Hungary, restored the line-up that won against France, with Schall in the 11 at the expense of Horvath, who had injured himself during the match against the Magyars. Italy, compared to the replay against Spain, made two changes. Both teams came in after two victories in which they didn't particularly shine. Austria's path hadn't been easy, neither against France nor against the Hungarians, and in both cases the Wunderteam had played extremely physical matches. Italy, for their part, after starting with a 7-1 win against the USA, then took two attempts to get past Spain. Meazza, the star of the *Azzurri*, arrived at the long-awaited match in good form: he had scored in the first match against Spain and had also been on target against the United States. His Austrian counterpart, Sindelar, had been in and out, scoring against France and then setting up Schall against Hungary but also spending a lot of inactive time in both ties. Sindelar, however, had seven more years of career experience in his legs than the Italian star.

The players took to the pitch under the orders of Swedish referee Eklind and on top in the early stages were the Wunderteam, with Sindelar apparently unaffected by a heavy pitch. When the Austrians attacked, Pozzo's defenders gave the impression that they were more concerned with pushing the opponent back than setting up a counter-attack. Italy were being cautious, and when they did counter they went through Schiavio. The decision to play the Bologna forward instead of Borel was probably based on his ability to assert his physical prowess, a quality that the small Juventus striker lacked. Schiavio had the first shot on goal, but Platzer was equal to it.

The Austrians returned to attack and the Italians' approach became even more limited: Sindelar was in a state of grace, dancing on the ball and always found a free partner. So Luis Monti decided to stamp it out with interventions often beyond the rules, but Eklind – who was also promised the final – seemed the only one who didn't realise what was happening. The only warning Monti received came shortly afterwards, when he knocked down Viertl in one of the numerous Austrian raids in the Italian half. Sindelar had already tasted the harshness of Italian defences in the semifinal of the 1933/34 Mitropa Cup, when first Monti himself – sent off in the 85th minute of the first leg in Vienna – and then Varglien and Calligaris had struggled to contain him.

Pozzo, who besides coaching the Italian national team also wrote in *La Stampa*, said of the clashes between

Sindelar and Monti, 'They didn't get along at all. It was mutual. It was one of those natural, instinctive, irresistible antipathies. The Viennese did not like Luisito's resolute, masculine character, and Luisito did not like the dances of the Austrian who seemed to want to make fun of him. Monti's unpopularity on the playing field was three-quarters due to the criticism he had received for knocking down an idol like Sindelar.'

Austria played some beautiful football at times but were struggling to unhinge the Italian defence and find the target. Italy were the opposite; less enjoyable to watch but more solid. Schiavio continued his personal duel with Platzer, but for the second time the goalkeeper came out on top. However, from the rebound, three Italian players homed in on the ball. Meazza and Platzer collided, Schiavio stopped his run right in front of Platzer and from behind he fed Guaita who dispatched the ball into the net. For the Austrians, the foul on the goalkeeper had been obvious; for Eklind it wasn't. The Italian defensive deadbolt solidified even more, now that they had a lead to hold on to. Austria had four chances to equalise but Combi stopped Viertl, Zischek, Bican and Schall. After a very intense first half, the teams went in for the interval.

Back on the pitch, the players continued the battle and Sindelar was now playing at half-pace. Monti's eagerness had almost put him out of the match, but after consulting with Meisl and his team-mates Sindelar had decided to return. For a quarter of an hour the game was dominated by nervousness until Schall had an attempt on goal, and then Cisar – not a prolific scorer – was also unsuccessful. The game became more fragmented and good chances were scarce. Italy had three opportunities to seal their progress: the first with Guaita after a raid in Austria's area, and then with Schiavio and Meazza. Platzer, however, was in as good form as Combi was and then Austria almost drew level after good work from Viertl and Schall.

With ten minutes to go, Austria pushed on in search of an equaliser but were regularly denied by Combi, while Platzer kept out Schiavio and Ferrari to prevent Italy from doubling their lead. Right at the end, Zischek had the chance to take the tie to extra time but his shot was off target. So Italy went through and Austria were out, meaning they had to face Germany in a play-off for third and fourth place.

Meisl's run of good results was interrupted by that defeat and after the game, the Austrian coach said:

'It happened exactly as I imagined. It was impossible to beat Italy in such a context. You have to surrender and give the title to the *Azzurri*. But that doesn't mean that their football is better and that the title was won deservedly.'

In later years, Josef Bican said:

'Thanks to Meisl we knew that the referee was corrupt and that he would arbitrate in favour of Italy. He even went so far as to play with them: at one point he passed the ball to the right wing, and one of my team-mates, Zischek, ran to reach him, but the referee returned it to the Italians. It was a disgrace.'

Raimundo Orsi, who had been part of the Italian 11 in that match, later claimed that he and his companions would have been in danger of the death penalty 'if Eklind had not been on our side'.

What is certain is that from a match officiating point of view, the domestic representation was sizeable: among the 25 referees and linesmen, 12 of them were Italian.

*Hugo Meisl during a training session. (erein für Geschichte der ArbeiterInnenbewegung - VGA, Vienna)*

*Meisl with the Wunderteam in Glasgow (Hugo Meisl Archiv Hafer)*

*Hugo Meisl and some Wunderteam members at a train station (Verein für Geschichte der ArbeiterInnenbewegung - VGA, Vienna)*

*The members of the Committee for the Mitropa Cup gathering in 1935. (Hugo Meisl Archiv Hafer)*

*The reserve formation of Hertha Vienna during season 1921/22. Matthias
Sindelar is fourth from the right (Bezirkmuseum Favoriten)*

*Sindelar with his sisters in 1922 (Bezirkmuseum Favoriten)*

*Sindelar during a match Austria played against Switzerland in 1932 (Bezirkmuseum Favoriten)*

*Sindelar wearing the Austria Vienna jersey in 1936. (Bezirkmuseum Favoriten)*

*Sindelar during a match played at the Hohe Warte stadium in 1936. (Bezirkmuseum Favoriten)*

*Sindelar wearing the Austria Vienna jersey in 1937 (Bezirkmuseum Favoriten)*

*Matthias Sindelar during an excursion with his family in 1937 (Bezirkmuseum Favoriten)*

*Sindelar in the role of movie actor in 1937 (Bezirkmuseum Favoriten)*

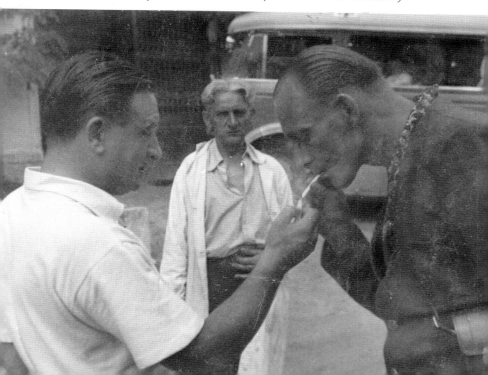

*The Wunderteam at the Prater stadium before a victory against Italy on 20 March 1932 (Verein für Geschichte der ArbeiterInnenbewegung - VGA, Vienna)*

*Austrian players show the Nazi salute before the Anschlussspiel in 1938 (Fussball Sonntag)*

*German and Austrian players' signatures to support the Anschluss (Fussball Sonntag)*

The Annahof renamed
Cafe Sindelar in
1939 (Bezirkmuseum
Favoriten)

Wegen Renovierung
GESCHLOSSEN!

ÜBERNAHME
durch Matthias
SINDELAR

Sindelar the day of the
opening of the Annahof
(Bezirkmuseum
Favoriten)

4

THE PLAY-OFF for third and fourth place was played on 7 June and saw Austria facing a German side that had exceeded expectations in reaching the semi-finals where they were beaten by the greater talent of the Czechoslovakian players, in particular the hat-trick scorer Oldrich 'Olda' Nejedlý.

Austria v Germany was the least-anticipated game of the entire World Cup; a classic consolation match worth nothing. It was not surprising that there were only 9,000 spectators at the Municipal Stadium in Naples, despite the fact that prices had been lowered to encourage greater attendance. That was only around one-fifth of the stadium's capacity. Only once before, 15 years previously, had Meisl seen his team playing in such an empty arena, for a friendly against Hungary. Absent from the play-off was Matthias Sindelar, who had mutually agreed with Meisl not to take part. The clashes with Monti had injured him and the two had agreed that it was not worth risking aggravating his problems in a game useful only for the almanacs. In Sindelar's place, Meisl picked Braun, and Horvath replaced Schall in attack.

During his 15-year adventure as the Wunderteam's coach, Hugo Meisl had faced Germany six times. Three of those had been wins, with two defeats and one draw. The most comforting point, however, was that when counting the last two fixtures, Austria had scored 11 goals with none conceded having won 6-0 in Berlin in May 1931 and 5-0 in Vienna in September of the same year. However, since that Vienna encounter, the teams had changed considerably. Only Zischek, Smistik and Schall remained for Austria.

The game began with Austria looking timid and unmotivated. In fact, the performance didn't really look like Austria. It had nothing of the Wunderteam, neither its leader nor its traditional white shirt. In order to avoid any confusion between the shirts of the two teams, Napoli had provided the Austrians with their own strips.

It took Germany only 25 seconds to take the lead as Ernst Lehrer scored the fastest goal in the then short history of the World Cup, a record that would be broken in 1962 by Czechoslovakia's Mašek against Mexico and later by Turkey's Hakan Şükür, who took 11 seconds to beat the South Korean goalkeeper in 2002.

Austria did not react and Germany doubled their lead through Edmund Conen, who was the tournament's joint second-highest goalscorer alongside Italy's Angelo Schiavio. Meisl's men had pride to play for and through Horvath, their best performer on the day, they halved their deficit. But that wouldn't be enough and the Austrians' defensive structure gave way for a third time when Lehrer took advantage of it and scored his second in the 42nd minute.

In the second half, Austria proved to be more strong-willed. And Sesta, better as an attacker than as a defender, reduced the gap again nine minutes in. Horvath, towards the end, went close to an equaliser, but his effort hit the post. Germany took third place but among the Austrian ranks the regret continued to be directed to the semi-final lost against the *Azzurri*. The criticism from the newspapers was ruthless. There were those who complained about the poor physical condition of the players, claiming that it was due to poor training and insufficient nutrition, and those who, like *Das Kleine Blatt*, accused Meisl of ignoring important players like Karl Gall and Josef Stroh.

In any case, it was clear that a cycle was over, and that one of the strongest national teams of the time would have to renew itself in order to be able to compete again at the top level. The 15 years of Hugo Meisl had led the side to be renamed the Wunderteam because of a sparkling style that reflected the personality and philosophy of its coach.

The Wunderteam would not have a chance of revenge at world level and in the 1938 finals some of the players who had taken part in Italy did reappear, but in another nation's shirt. Sindelar's and his team-mates' ambitions had been shattered against Italy by refereeing that many still call suspicious. The same feeling was denounced by some Czechoslovakia players who would lose the final against Italy a few days later.

# VIII

# THE CONNECTION
# GAME AND THE END
# OF THE WUNDERTEAM

*On 15 March 1938, from a balcony in the Neue Hofburg on Heldenplatz and in front of about 250,000 people, Adolf Hitler delivered the historic speech that made official the annexation of Austria – which the Germans renamed Ostmark – to the Third Reich. A little less than a month later, a referendum was held to ask the Austrian and German citizens whether they were in favour of annexation. In fact, as the election question itself stated, the annexation had already taken place and had already been announced. The referendum was a move by the National Socialists to legitimise their rise to power. The days before the Anschluss had seen some influential Viennese figures working to promote the National Socialist cause. Theodor Innitzer, archbishop of the Austrian capital who a few years later condemned the persecution of Jews and gypsies, was such a long-time supporter of the Anschluss that in April 1938, to celebrate the Führer's birthday, he ordered all the churches in the city to adorn themselves with flags bearing the swastika symbol. On a sporting level, football became amateur once again. Some immediate effects were the withdrawal from the Mitropa Cup by the Austrian teams and the suspension of the International Cup. It had only taken a handful of hours for the Nazis to destroy what Hugo Meisl had built in previous years.*

# 1

IN 1918, when the Great War came to an end, the Austrian people were divided over their future. There were those who dreamed of a republican, independent and Catholic Austria, and those who, like the supporters of the Grossdeutsche Volkspartei, hoped for the union of Austria with the Weimar Republic in the name of the Pan-Germanist theories that had sprung up at the end of the previous century.

However, in 1919 the Treaty of Saint-Germain-en-Laye not only redesigned the borders of the country, but also prohibited the latter move. This decision gave rise to the First Republic of Austria, which would continue until 1933, the year in which Engelbert Dollfuss founded the Vaterländische Front, creating a corporate dictatorship better known as Ständestaat.

The following year, Dollfuss banned the Social Democrats, the KPÖ – Kommunistische Partei Österreichs – the Austrian Communist Party, and the DNSAP, the National Socialist Party, from parliament.

From 12 to 15 February 1934 a violent civil war broke out between the Heimwehr, the militia supporting Chancellor Dollfuss, and the Schutzbund, a paramilitary organisation representing the Social Democrats. The revolt was quelled, but the tensions would continue and extend to the National Socialist movement which, on 25 July 1934, assassinated the Austrian Chancellor when some of its members entered the Chancellery building and shot him. Germany, however, denied any involvement in the attack.

Kurt Von Schuschnigg, who took over from Dollfuss, had to cope with even greater pressure: on 22 February 1938 he was summoned by Hitler to the Führer's mountain residence in Berchtesgaden. Hitler informed the new Austrian Chancellor of his desire to annex Austria to Germany, and in response Von Schuschnigg called a referendum. It would be the people who would decide. From Berlin, Goebbels proposed an alternative: he asked the Chancellor to postpone the referendum for two weeks and to resign in favour of Arthur Seyss-Inquart, an Austrian National Socialist. Von Schuschnigg did not resign but agreed to hold the referendum two weeks later.

However, threats and pressure increased and Von Schuschnigg decided to leave his post. President Willhem Miklas, after some initial resistance, ended up giving in and appointed Seyss-Inquart as head of the Chancellery. On 12 March, German troops began marching to Austria, and two days later Hitler reached Vienna. On 10 April 1938, the referendum was held in both Germany and Austria, and the verdict was unanimous: 99.73 per cent of the voters voted in favour of annexation, and Austria, renamed Ostmark, became a province of the Third Reich.

2

JUST A few weeks after the Anschluss, Vienna had already become decidedly more 'Prussian' – a term with which the Austrians used to refer to the Germans – and the attempt to replace the classic Viennese light-heartedness with German rigour was felt throughout the country. Officers of the SA patrolled the capital and the so-called 'Schupos', a derogatory term for policemen, watched over the imminent referendum.

This led to a drastic reorganisation of the football system with some inevitable consequences: on 14 March 1938 – only two days after the German invasion of Austria – Hakoah Vienna, together with all the remaining Jewish clubs, were dismantled with the consequent cancellation of the Austrian Cup match that Hakoah were to play against Simmering. The only exception was Maccabi Vienna, who remained for some time unscathed by the harassment imposed by Berlin. Several Jewish players from the banned teams ended up at Maccabi Vienna. Austria Vienna, who also had numerous Jewish leaders in their ranks, suffered the same fate when almost all of their members left the country while the club was banned and subjected to 'extraordinary administration'. Bruno Eckerl, a lawyer who remained in office until 1945 and who became a member of the National Socialist Party in 1941, took over as club president.

A similar fate befell the Jewish sports journalists, who were also purged of their jobs. The city's women's football clubs were not spared either: some of them, such as Admira, Tempo, Vienna, Wien and Vindobona, whose owner Josef Osovsky had property and assets totalling Deutsch Marks 2.2 million confiscated, were dismantled.

More generally, the entire Austrian football movement would be subject to the drastic changes imposed by Berlin: in Germany, in order to avoid the risk that football could become professional, the Nazi Party had tried at first to reduce the number of sports clubs and get athletes to join organisations affiliated to the National Socialist movement such as the SA, SS, Hitler Youth and Kraft Durch Freude, which translated as 'Strength Through Joy'.

But the impact that football had had on the German working classes and its conversion into a mass phenomenon, which had also happened in Austria, had led the Nazi leadership to reconsider their scepticism and to positively assess the impact that sport could have on the crowds. It was because of these considerations that Berlin hosted the Olympic Games in 1936. Furthermore, football also had a second important role: it offered the male population a few scraps of freedom and some distraction from the daily routine.

In this historical phase, a widespread tendency among Austrian clubs was to claim their past or their National Socialist identity, as at Wiener Sportklub, the only club that did not accept Jewish players or managers into its ranks even before 1938. Those clubs that could not boast of such connections tried to make up for it by recruiting members of the SA, SS or NSDAP, as did Rapid Vienna by appointing Otto Steinhäus, the chief of police of Vienna, as honorary president, and offering the sports director and deputy mayor

THE CONNECTION GAME AND THE END OF THE WUNDERTEAM

of Vienna, Thomas Kozich, an honorary gold badge. The WAC did the same with Otto Smolik, a district officer in the Austrian capital who had been a member of the then illegal National Socialist Party since well before 1938. The advantage was mutual: on the one hand the party could boast links with the most prestigious clubs in the city, and on the other hand, thanks to the presence among their ranks of influential personalities, the clubs could obtain favours such as allowing their players to postpone their departure to the front – starting in 1939 – or to stay around Vienna to take part in league matches. A further advantage was the possibility of preventing their young athletes from joining the ranks of the Hitler Youth or other similar organisations.

A 'racial conscience' was introduced into Austrian football for the first time. Many small teams were dismantled as their playing fields would be used for army training. In schools, on the other hand, the game of football was less harassed and even more encouraged.

All this had meant that the prospect and ambition of young people to become champions and play for their team or defend the colours of their national side had dropped considerably. There were fewer and fewer children playing football in the streets of Vienna. In this regard, *Sport-Tagblatt* wrote:

'For decades, young boys used their mothers' stockings to assemble soccer balls, at a time when every street in the city had its "Horvath", "Schindi" or "Uridil" and children showed their excellent technique on the streets. Today, our youth no longer feel the need to practise their favourite sport due to changed circumstances.'

Already in 1938, at the end of the spring season, the Reich had focused on its primary objective, the abolition of Austrian professional football. To this end, the regime took care to provide each player with a new profession.

Several articles appeared in the newspapers portraying some current and former players in their new occupations. One of them showed Sindelar working at his cafeteria, Annahof, and read, 'Sindi takes care of his customers.' In another one, Wilhelm Hahnemann was shown at a municipal office working in support of the disabled and it was reported, 'Precise and accurate, both in the penalty area and when typing.' Stefan Skoumal, who was a carpenter, was described thus, 'It is not surprising that his passages are as accurate as the wooden beams cut to perfection,' and Josef 'Pepi' Stroh, who worked at a petrol station, was pictured in a photo above which the phrase 'sells gasoline and signs autographs' stood out. Other players who found or were assigned a job were Hans Pesser, Karl Adamek, Franz Binder, Johann Mock, Anton Schall, Karl Sesta and Karl Zischek. The last two, like Sindelar, had received a licence to open a coffee shop.

Football thus returned to the amateur model and the Austrian championship was converted into a regional championships whereby the winners would face the winners of the other Gauligen, the highest level of German football between 1933 and 1945. The 1938 edition of the Tschammerpokal, the German Cup which had been named after the Minister Tschammer und Osten, was to be attended by the eight best Austrian teams, although the format was to change from the following year and include fewer teams. In Germany, clubs that were reluctant to comply with the dictates of amateur football were in danger of being banned. This, for example, was the sanction that Schalke 04 risked in the autumn of 1930. Curiously, within a few years, Schalke would become the most popular team in the Reich and consequently the one with which the National Socialist regime would be most reflected. In addition, several Austrian players and coaches moved to Altreich from the Anschlussspiel: Josef

Uridil, for example, the former star of SK Rapid and the Austrian national team during the 1920s, went to coach the German team Schwarz-Weiß Essen.

Little is known about the players' feelings towards the Anschluss and the National Socialist Party. Many had never publicly aired their views, or had instead declared themselves apolitical. The National Socialist Party, before it was banned, was in any case an established reality within the Austrian Parliament. It is not to be ignored that some Austrian players, most of whom had grown up on the outskirts of the capital where the workers' movements were rooted, did not see the annexation to Germany and the rise of National Socialism as a consequence.

One man who didn't make a secret of his National Socialist inclinations was Johann Mock, known as Hans. As Franz Schwarz, son of the former president of Austria Vienna, Emanuel Schwarz, revealed in an interview in 2008, Mock had already been a member of the then illegal SA and NSDAP (National Socialist German Workers' Party) in the years before 1938. From 1938 onwards he would regularly appear at his team's training camp wearing an SA bracelet. He, more than anyone else, would not hesitate to accept the call of the German national team for the upcoming World Cup.

# 3

LESS THAN a month after the annexation of Austria to the Reich, the Minister of Sport of the National Socialist government, Hans Von Tschammer und Osten, organised a friendly to seal the merger of the two football associations: der *Anschlussspiel*, as it was called, the match of the connection, a showcase to admire the Wunderteam and its players, who, if they agreed to join the German national squad, would take part in the upcoming World Cup to be held in France.

Sepp Herberger, the Germans' coach, was aware that tapping in to the Wunderteam could mean creating a perfect mix between the physical and athletic vigour of the Germans and the avant-garde football expressed by the Austrians. The challenge of combining two such different styles would be welcomed by the German coach as in 1930, when he was studying in Berlin, he wrote a thesis on the importance of combination football and a passing game. The event was scheduled for 3 April.

Compared to the golden years of the Wunderteam, some key figures were missing. Anton Schall, now 31 years old, was suffering from a cardiac anomaly that severely limited his performance; Josef Bican had fled to Czechoslovakia the year before, while Karl Zischek and Camillo Jerusalem both emigrated to France where they would stay for a few years. Walter Nausch had also packed his bags: he and his wife Margoth, a Jewish swimmer from Hakoah, had fled to Switzerland where Nausch would start playing for the Grasshoppers and then become Karl Rappan's assistant. The Reich leadership had actually offered him a contract to coach a regional team on the condition that he divorced his wife, but the player had refused.

For Germany that was a sports party, not a battle against an enemy to be defeated. Moreover, it was an opportunity for Herberger to see some of the most respected European players of that era who would have strengthened the ranks of the German national team.

In Berlin and in the local press, almost nobody was opposed to the possibility of creating a more inclusive national team that would also include Ostmark players, despite the fact that some of them were of Bohemian origin and, therefore, not exactly in line with the Aryan ideal. Winning matches took precedence over everything and would have justified any choice. Moreover, during the 1936 Olympic Games in Berlin, Aryan superiority in sport had already been disavowed when the African-American athlete Jesse Owens had beaten the German Luz Long in the long jump. Hitler had stood up and, in admiration, had applauded the exploits of the American athlete, contrary to the expectations of bystanders.

For some players of the now-declining Wunderteam, that match was an indispensable showcase to climb in the estimation of the German coach in view of the upcoming World Cup. For others, the motivations were more patriotic in nature and were aimed at reaffirming the superiority of Austrian football.

The match began at the orders of the 50-year-old referee Alfred Birlem, a German, and an old acquaintance of both teams having taken charge of a World Cup match in 1934 and having been the second official for the quarter-final between Austria and Hungary.

That day, the Vienna Prater was dotted with swastika flags. It looked more like Berlin or Nuremberg than Vienna, and one of the reasons was that only seven days later the referendum was to be held – the referendum with the already announced outcome.

To promote the event, the German propaganda media had used the image of some of the most popular athletes. *Völkischer Beobachter*, for example, published an image of Sindelar on the very day of the referendum, under which the handwritten sentence stood out, 'We players thank our Führer from the bottom of our hearts and will vote YES!' On the same day, an article entitled 'We and 600,000 other German players will vote YES' appeared in the *Fussball-Sonntag*, accompanied by the signatures of the 22 players who would play the match.

The stands were packed with 60,000 spectators. The Nazi general staff had set up in the grandstands. Among those present were Hans Von Tschammer, Richard Eberstaller – the now former secretary of the ÖFB, who had a past as a member of the then illegal National Socialist Party, DFB president Felix Linnemann, and Seyss-Inquart, who would remain in office to sign the Constitutional Law. Contrary to some rumours that would spread further afield over the years, there was no Adolf Hitler, who was in Graz to personally support a campaign in favour of the Anschluss.

To differentiate themselves from their rivals, the Wunderteam wore for the first time an all-red shirt with no white borders or details, as any reference to Austria and its flag would have to disappear. For this reason the double eagle, the symbol of the nation that had regularly appeared on Austrian shirts until that day, was also missing. Germany lined up in their white uniform. It was Sunday and the typical spring weather reigned, ideal for such an occasion.

The Wunderteam's line-up was: Platzer, Schmaus, Sesta, Wagner, Mock, Skoumal, Hahnemann, Stroh, Sindelar, Binder, Pesser.

Germany lined up with: Jakob, Janes, Münzenberg, Kupfer, Goldbrunner, Kitzinger, Lehner, Gellesch, Berndt, Gauchel, Fath.

Germany took the field with eight out of 11 members of the 'Breslau-Elf', a nickname that the national team had earned after a 9-0 friendly victory against Denmark played in the Polish city of Wroclaw, then under German control. For its part, the Austrians lined up with a different formation compared to the one that had taken the field during the last match: seven changes were made. One of the new recruits was Matthias Sindelar, who had been injured during a championship match in 1937 and had recently returned to the ranks.

Seven of the Austrian players would later be called up by Herberger for the World Cup; three would not be part of the French expedition but would play some friendly matches in the following years and only one, Matthias Sindelar, would never wear the shirt of the German national team.

The game began and from the stands, crowded with red-white-black flags, came applause for the players of both sides. In the early minutes the German players were on top. Their physical vigour and athletic approach got the better of their opponents and Platzer was forced to make two big saves. Sindelar seemed to be out on his feet but, aged 35 and with a battered knee, his form could not always be at its peak. Nevertheless, as the minutes went by, the technique and fluidity of the Austrians' game began to show and Sindelar himself missed a chance that a player of his calibre should have taken. Then it was Franz Binder's turn: the SK Rapid centre-forward hit a 25-yard shot that Regensburg goalkeeper Jakob struggled with but kept out. A few minutes later, Ostmark hit the bar and Binder was unable to finish off the rebound. From the stands you could hear the chorus, 'Binder wake up!' The day after the match, the Viennese newspapers were not kind to their centre-forward. *Sport-Tagblatt*, for example, would write, 'Binder tortured the spectators.' The first half ended at 0-0.

During the interval, two of the Austrian team's reserves, FK Austria goalkeeper Rudolf Zöhrer and Admira defender Otto Marischka, walked around the pitch holding up a sign saying 'Sportsmen Vote YES'. Then it was the turn of the speeches: after a brief talk by the new mayor of Vienna Hermann Neubacher it was the turn of Hans Tschammer und Osten, who took the microphone in his hand and said, 'Dear Viennese football supporters and friends of football in general, dear football community! I read that Austrian football would die. I would like to state that this is a great lie. I also declare that Austrian football will survive, and will do so alongside German football. The art of Viennese football and the Vienna School are unique in the world, we would be foolish to want to destroy it. Therefore, Viennese football will survive, as will the players you are seeing today. Today represents a historic moment in the development of German football life. When the game is over, the German players will shake hands with their Austrian colleagues. Thus, German sport will work together with Austrian sport eternally for the great Reich. Our people must also be united in sport. Long live Germany, German sport and the Führer!'

The second half began like the first, with the Germans threatening Platzer's goal, but after a few minutes Austria took the lead when Sindelar scored after Binder had hit the post.

That changed the game and with a very powerful strike from about 45 metres, Sesta doubled the lead and sealed the 2-0 win. 'Der Papierene' and 'Der Blader', the 'Man of Cartavelina' and the 'Fat Man', as Sindelar and Sesta were nicknamed, were the two decisive players – the pair who perhaps less than anyone else represented the ideal of the Aryan athlete mythologised by Goebbels's propaganda.

That was the second goal for the Austria Vienna defender for his national team, both against Germany and both from outside the penalty area. *Neue Wiener Tagblatt* called that feat 'a stroke of luck', blaming the goalkeeper Jakob who had found himself too far out of his goal. *Völkischer Beobachter* instead praised Sesta as the best player of the game. In addition to the goal, the newspaper wrote that the Austrian had 'almost single-handedly' blocked the German attacks on the left side. Within the same article, the journalist also dwelt on other individual performances, such as those of Sindelar and Stroh, who had shown 'great technique and excellent physical condition'.

But not everyone agreed on Sindelar's performance. *Neue Wiener Tagblatt*, the newspaper that more than any other had belittled the performance of the Austrians, claimed that both Sindelar and Binder, despite contributing to the first goal, had not been at the level of their team-mates.

4

SINCE THE end of the war, many myths about the *Anschlussspiel* were reported and have spread to the present day. They had appeared in the press before and in recent years have found their way on to the blogs of enthusiasts around the world. The narrative created was important to the Austrians' need to distance themselves from the war years and the resulting barbarism. Many were the stories of resistance that had been brought to light, some of which had been matched by authentic national heroes. One of them was the Viennese Anton Schmid, who had been shot in Vilnius in 1942 because, as a soldier of the Wehrmacht, he had helped 250 Jewish men, women and children to avoid the concentration camps by providing them with false documents and, in some cases, allowing them to escape from Lukiski prison.

In later years, these events would also involve the world of sport. The figure who lent himself to this better than any other was Matthias Sindelar. Sindelar, from this point of view, represented an extremely expendable character: he had never worn the shirt of the German national team, he had spent almost all of his career with FK Austria, a club linked to the city's Jewish bourgeoisie and had excellent relations with the top management of his society, as testified by the letter he had written to his former president Emanuel Schwarz the day he was forced to leave his office. Moreover, Sindelar was for all

212

the greatest example of the *Scheiberlspiel*, the style of play that Meisl had imprinted on his national team, and the leading figure behind the successes of the side.

Here, however, verifiable and proven historical facts are interrupted and legends begin before going around the world from Vienna.

The first inaccuracy put into circulation concerned the atmosphere that had preceded the *Anschlussspiel*: someone claimed that the final result should have been a victory for Germany; someone else, instead, talked about an announced draw. According to proponents of the first theory, a German victory would have highlighted the superiority of the motherland over the province, and a draw would have made everyone happy. The truth was that the Third Reich had not bothered in any way to favour one result at the expense of another. The ups and downs of the game had shown this: the Germans had made a good start against the Austrians, who, strengthened by their technical superiority, had brought home the victory. In addition, it was clear from Herberger's archives that Linnemann had told the German players that, although it was an important game, a victory should have arrived without contrasts or hard interventions. Herberger wrote, 'We couldn't have done the Austrians a bigger favour,' since the team led by Sindelar was clearly superior. Günther Doubek, who was only ten years old at the time and had watched the match from sector A of the stadium, said, 'When a player fell, an opponent immediately helped him to get up. Just like us guys do when we play on the Ottakring field.'

With regard to the behaviour of the fans, historians and reporters were divided: there were those who reported, like Wolfgang Maderthaner, a large presence in the stands of members of the Party and SA, SS and Wehrmacht who would occupy entire sectors, while others had shown a good representation of Austrian fans who had come to support their compatriots ardently against the 'piefkes', a disdain with which the Germans were defined.

The second myth concerned the shirt in which Austria had appeared. Someone erroneously claimed that Austria had worn a red top for the first time, and that this decision had been taken by Matthias Sindelar. In fact, the Austrians had already worn red on at least three occasions, notably in the 1930, 1932 and 1936 friendlies against England. The peculiarity of the shirt worn that day, if anything, was the absence of any reference to the Austrian flag.

Even the goal that unlocked the match was often described in a misleading way: many people reported a spectacular shot that Sindelar would have scored from 30 metres, while in reality the strike had been from within the penalty area and was relatively normal for a striker of his level. Evidence of this are the drawings of *Sport-Montag* magazine, made the day after the match.

A few moments later, again according to the stories that were to proliferate in the years following the end of the war, Sindelar entertained fans with a ballet in front of the grandstand occupied by the Nazi general staff. Nothing could be more false: Sindelar and Sesta simply celebrated together. Matthias Sindelar, among other things, was well aware that this would be his last international appearance before his public. Two celebrations and nothing more, as *Ostmark-Wochenschau-Bericht* confirmed the day after the match. The news report described Sindelar jumping with joy surrounded by his team-mates for a few seconds before heading for the midfield circle.

*Völkischer Beobachter* wrote instead that Sindelar had approached the grandstand where the Nazi comrades were sitting, and that they were doing so for a propaganda promotion of the event. Günther Doubek gave some additional details, claiming that although Sindelar's reaction had taken place in front of sector B, where the grandstand was also located, the gesture may have been quietly addressed to the 100 or so Austrian fans who populated the upper grandstand and had been greeted with the chorus 'Sindi! Sindi!'

When it was time to award the medals and prizes, players approached the centre circle in single file to greet the officers. When the Nazi salute was ordered, accompanied by the cry 'Heil Hitler', only two of the 22 players did not respond as requested: Sindelar and Sesta. The latter, not being protected by the fame and reputation of his famous colleague, served two weeks in prison. There is, however, no visual or printed evidence that would corroborate this course of events. Once again, *Völkischer Beobachter*'s chronicler gave an accurate account of those moments:

'After performing the Nazi salute, the players shook hands halfway down the pitch and marched off, chanting blaring choirs under the grandstand. There Sindelar received the congratulations of the Reich's sports director and after a "Sieg Heil" addressed to the sports director, the teams moved away from the field while being cheered on by the fans.'

Sindelar's statements at the end of the match focused only on what he said was a deserved victory for the Austrians:

'It was a quick and enjoyable game that reached its highest point at the start of the second half. We did more to get the victory. The Germans showed good exchanges, but found it difficult to get into the area. I'm very happy with the team's performance, we all gave our best. We're very happy that the last match of the Austrian-German team coincided with a victory.'

Even the reaction from the newspapers appeared dampened and focused on what had happened on the pitch, without emphasising anything else. The Austrian newspapers celebrated the feat with enthusiastic tones, while the German ones played down the defeat with headlines such as 'German football flourishes in Austria', 'The national team comes out defeated by an excellent game' and 'Here is the 11 from Austria in view of the World Cup'. Few focused on the superiority of the Wunderteam, although *Neue Freie Presse* wrote, 'Triumph of the Viennese football school'. The *Völkischer Beobachter*, on the other hand, argued that the goal of the meeting had been achieved: it had guaranteed excellent publicity in view of the forthcoming referendum.

## IX

# THE 1938 WORLD CUP
# AND THE CALL TO ARMS

*Only a few months before the departure of the German national team for the World Cup in France, young coach Sepp Herberger was facing plenty of questions from the newspapers. Which method of play to use? The notorious Viennese pyramid devised by Meisl or the German W-M scheme? A style of play centred on strength, as was tradition in Germany, or the Austrian one, based instead on the* Scheiberlspiel *and more suited to favour individuality and short passages? Or maybe a mixture of the two? The answers came via a confrontation with the top management of the DFB. In those months, newspapers had often said that the two different styles reflected two different ways of understanding life: on the one hand was the* Wiener Schmäh, *the Viennese philosophy according to which life should not be taken too seriously, and on the other hand the German mentality, more linked to concepts such as seriousness and application. Herberger knew that in the event of failure he would not be spared criticism from the top. But he also knew that a victory would mean an absolute justification of his work. However,*

*Germany had finished third in 1934 under Otto Nerz – who later resigned from his post after his disappointing outcome at the 1936 Olympic Games.*

# 1

THE RIVALRY between Austrian and German football at the highest began in 1938, when the best Viennese and German clubs – now both under the aegis of the Third Reich – began to play each other in the German championship and Tschammerpokal.

The Anschluss, at a sporting level, would also have represented the fusion between two different footballing styles. During life at the battle front, playing football had taken root mainly among German soldiers who had been deployed in the less beaten areas of the Western Front. The fact that soccer had sprouted at a time when life and death were connected even more so than normal had shaped some of its characteristics, such as a strong emphasis on physical confrontation. From 1919 onwards it became the sport of the proletariat and spread among the university fraternities, giving rise to ceremonial events such as the 'Salamander', the practice of getting drunk after matches.

Compared to what had happened in Austria, German football was never restricted to a city. In the various regions of the Third Reich, the Gauligen, the regional championships, were held, at the end of which the winners competed in the German championship, which included first rounds and then knockout rounds. The regional nature of German football was also reflected in the composition of the teams. While the Viennese line-ups included a good number of players whose families came from different corners of the empire, the German sides were often represented by domestic players who were born and raised in a particular region and city, who spoke the local dialect fluently and were therefore able to develop an affinity with their fans. When Schalke 04 faced Admira Vienna in the final of the German championship in 1939, the Schalke side contained an 11 exclusively composed of players born within the Ruhr, the Gelsenkirchen region. Among them was Kalwitski, the match's star striker, and Schalke 04's historic front-men Fritz Szepan and Ernst Kuzorra.

The 1930s had seen the domination of German football by Schalke 04, the most popular team in the Reich and the sporting pride of a nation that had never shone internationally. Thus, 'Schalker Kreisel' was born, a style of play more similar to the Austrian one than the one traditionally in vogue among German clubs.

Before 1938 there had not been too many meetings between the two national teams. They were nearly always friendlies and did not even have as much of an edge as those between the Austrian, Hungarian, Italian and Czechoslovakian sides.

Their first game since the end of the Great War was on 26 September 1920 and ended 3-2 in favour of the Austrians, thanks to Jakob Swatosch's hat-trick. Other noteworthy encounters were the 6-0 and 5-0 victories in favour of Meisl's men during the golden age of the Wunderteam.

Then there was the play-off for third and fourth place at the 1934 World Cup, won by Germany, but even that was not enough to establish who really held the upper hand between the two teams. After years of frozen institutional relations between the two countries came the *Anschlussspiel* of 1938, whose symbolic and political value went far beyond sport.

On a continental level, the Austrian Wunderteam enjoyed a better reputation. Containing Matthias Sindelar and playing in the style conceived by Hugo Meisl and Jimmy Hogan, the Wunderteam had been among the favourites for the 1934 World Cup and their players were known to the general public for winning the International Cup in 1932 and for the successes achieved by some of them with their clubs in the Mitropa Cup. The German clubs, having never taken part in the Mitropa Cup, were still an unknown factor on the European scene.

In 1938 the matches between German and Austrian clubs began and on 8 June 1939, in a fixture celebrating the 40th anniversary of the foundation of Rapid, they saw off the German champions Hannover 96 with a roaring score of 11-1. Their superiority seemed clear to everyone, despite *Reichssportblatt* trying to play down the extent of this defeat by talking about 'victory deserved by the most experienced team'. From then on, the meetings between the Austrian and German sides intensified during the competitions organised by the Third Reich.

Internationally, the German style of play had already received harsh criticism at home two years earlier, following the team's elimination from the Olympic Games. Otto Nerz had ended up in the dock, guilty according to the players and press of too much on strength and speed, with training that some came to call 'military'. Karl Hohmann, a centre-forward in that side, had declared, 'We didn't have time to do anything else.'

Later, Sepp Herberger, who succeeded Nerz, had given new life to the national team by promoting some less physical but more technical players, such as the centre-forward Fritz Szepan.

# 2

THE WUNDERTEAM had broken up and would not have a second chance to compete for the World Cup. However, some players did, while instead wearing the white shirt of Germany.

Of the 11 players who had beaten Germany in the *Anschlussspiel*, most were summoned by Herberger for the World Cup in France and few refused the invitation. The seven Austrian players selected were Mock, Stroh, Hahnemann, Skoumal, Pesser, Schmaus and Wagner. In reserve were goalkeeper Rudolf Raftl and the 19-year-old Leopold Neumer. Franz Binder, however, was not selected. The reason for this was probably tactical. Binder was an extraordinary centre-forward but was not very versatile, unlike Hahnemann for example. And already in the role was the indispensable Szepan, a star of Germany's most popular team, Schalke. And not all of the Austrian players would have been Herberger's first choices.

The coach had succeeded in strengthening Germany by drawing on the most decorated Austrian players. But Herberger had failed in his repeated attempts to convince Matthias Sindelar to be part of that project. In those months, in Vienna, there were rumours of private meetings between Sindelar and Herberger aimed at making the Austrian re-evaluate his reluctance. But Sindelar seemed unwilling and his appearances in the Austrian team had drastically decreased since well before the Anschluss, due to repeated knee problems.

So Herberger found himself having to revolutionise his starting plans: the young coach, in an authentic document written in pencil and with notes in the margins, claimed, 'Sindelar's name will always remain linked to the success and fame of the Austrian national team. Over time it became the emblem of that style of play called the Vienna School. However, I cannot ignore the fact that his performance has declined due to his age. When I stayed in Vienna, the leaders of the Austria team all claimed Sindelar's problem was the age! I cannot, however, ignore his successes, although he explicitly asked me on the phone not to be summoned.'

However, the way that document was drafted suggested that Herberger, at least at first, was certain that he could count on Sindelar: in all formations the 2-3-5 appeared with Sindelar as the centrepiece. Herberger was among the first in Germany to distance himself from the W-M scheme in favour of the Viennese pyramid. In later years, that same system would take root among different German teams. In an interview in March 1941, the Bavarian sports manager Oberhuber described the system as pioneering, and he said that some clubs such as Nürnberg, Fürth and Augsburg would have to adopt it. According to him, the figure of the stopper instead of a central midfielder was an 'English disease' and therefore the 3-2-2-3 typically adopted by the Germans had to be abandoned.

The very first formation sketched by Herberger presented the goalkeeper, defence and midfield of Germany and the attacking line of Austria, which besides Sindelar included Stroh, Neumer, Hahnemann and Binder. In a side note, Herberger had written, 'Szepan is out of shape.' Herberger then recounted that the DFB – through the Sportgauführer Freidrich Rainer – had organised two friendly matches, one against Aston Villa and the other against the English national team ahead of the World Cup. In one case Herberger was going to field a purely German formation and in the other with an 11 entirely composed of Austrian players. Nerz informed him of this decision, claiming that Tschammer und Osten wanted to see both Sindelar and Sesta at work. In his notes, however, Herberger pointed out that while Sindelar was a fixture for him, Sesta was not a priority, denouncing his stormy character.

A team-mate of Karl Sesta's would tell years later about a violent quarrel between the defender and the German coach. During a training session in which both German and Austrian players had taken part, following a call from his coach, a nervous Sesta replied, 'Idiot, you've never played football, how can you expect to teach us how to play? You can only watch us!'

Ostmark then played a friendly in Krefeld, a small German town, in front of about 500 spectators. One of them was Herberger, who had approached Sindelar shortly after the match and tried to convince him again. But once again it was to no avail, so much so that the coach wrote in his notes, 'Like in Vienna!', referring to the first refusal by the player.

About 30 years later, Herberger claimed to have had the impression that, although Sindelar had not communicated it explicitly to him, the refusal would have been due to the fact that the player felt a certain unease about the political events surrounding him and therefore did not want to represent the Third Reich. And when the German national team – composed entirely of Austrian players – faced Aston Villa in Berlin, Sindelar did not take the field.

One of the orders that the DFB imposed on Herberger was to select a team with five Austrians and six Germans or vice-versa. Herberger learned of that diktat after a meeting in Szczecin – now part of Poland – where Felix Linnemann, as spokesman for the DFB, had told him about this decision, claiming that it was the Führer's will. Herberger, although against it, had considered convening a majority of Austrian forwards alongside German defenders and midfielders as the forwards would be more easily integrated into a new system of play. Between 1938 and 1945, 116 Austrian players were summoned to the ranks of the German national team, 73 of whom were forwards.

One of Herberger's main fears was the internal divisions between Austrian and German players. In one of the first training sessions after the Anschluss there was a fight between the German forward Fritz Szepan and the Austrian Joseph Stroh: Stroh had performed a prolonged dribble with right, left and head in front of Szepan, receiving the applause of his Austrian team-mates, and in response Szepan had repeated the same dribble before throwing the ball into the net, arousing the approval of the German players. Because of this and other skirmishes, the coach worked to ensure that these obstacles were overcome by confronting the more mature and experienced German players including Münzenberg, Goldbrunner, Janes and Lehner. He also talked to Szepan, whose attitude was often irreverent, and the Austrians Schmaus and Mock, having the impression that he had managed to gain the co-operation of both sides.

# 3

THE FRENCH edition of the World Cup maintained a format quite similar to the Italian one: a large number of stadiums capable of hosting matches, 16 teams playing straight knockout matches – in the first post-war edition, in 1950, the format would change substantially – and replays in case of drawn matches even after extra time (penalty shoot-outs had not yet been introduced).

Uruguay and Argentina declined to take part as they favoured an alternation between Europe and South America in the hosting of the event, which had not happened. Germany had also applied to hold the tournament but won no votes, partly because it had already hosted the Olympic Games two years earlier and partly because the FIFA leadership did not want the National Socialist regime to use the event for propaganda, as had happened in Italy only four years earlier. The most formidable South American contender was therefore Brazil, which came back with its number one ace: Leônidas.

France was chosen as the host nation, in whose capital only ten years earlier the Briand-Kellogg Pact had been signed, named after the French mediator Briand and the US mediator Kellogg, through which the great powers had pledged not to use war to settle disputes and conflicts.

Austria were missing because of the Anschluss, although they had actually qualified after winning 2-1 against Latvia thanks to Franz Binder's decisive goal. The ÖFB had chosen Ludwig 'Luigi' Hussak, the former Amateure star of the early 20th century, as the national team's technical trainer for the World Cup. Hussak formed three teams that would then help him choose the squad: the starting 11, the second group and a selection of promising youngsters. The football geography, compared to only a few years before, had radically changed and neither of the two finalists of 1930, nor the team considered favourites for the 1934 event, competed at the 1938 World Cup. As a result, Sweden, who had been drawn to face Austria in the last 16, went directly to the quarter-finals. Defending champions Italy were there, as well as other central European powers in Hungary and Czechoslovakia. France, although not one of the favourites, were considered by all to be a better proposition than their 1934 side. The Austrian player Auguste Jordan, who had landed in France in 1933 and had obtained a French passport, was among their squad. The former Wunderteam goalkeeper Rudolf Hiden had also followed the same path, becoming Rodolphe. However, Rodolphe would only make one appearance for France, in 1940.

4

AGAINST ALL expectations, however, the 'Germany of the Austrians' were unable to get past Switzerland in the first knockout round. Herberger had decided to field five Austrian players – Raftl, Schmaus, Mock, Hahnemann and Pesser – against the unfancied Swiss.

The first attempt to settle the tie had finished a disappointing 1-1 with Gauchel's goal cancelled out by the Swiss striker Abegglen. One of the Austrian players, Hans Pesser, was the main target of the German press the day after the match: he had been sent off for a foul in the first half, and for the Reich newspapers that episode had exacerbated the bitterness of the fans towards the national team. Pesser, who had also been disqualified for any other matches in that competition, was suspended from the national team for two months following Felix Linnemann's request. Pesser's problems with the German national team had started before his arrival in France: he had been one of the players who had struggled most to comply with the hard routine imposed by Herberger, who favoured waking up at eight o'clock in the morning and training sessions that would start shortly afterwards. Herberger was also not exempt from criticism: the newspapers had blamed him for laying Hahnemann out of position.

The coach seemed extremely worried, fearing the reaction from Berlin in the event of an early exit, and was thinking of changing his formation for the replay. He was also aware that a national team aiming to win the World Cup would have been expected to beat Switzerland without too much trouble, especially as tougher tests would come in later rounds. The replay took place five days later. In the meantime, the main title contenders had all reached the quarter-finals.

The 20,000 spectators who went to the Parc des Princes were all rooting for Switzerland, as were the 27,000 who had attended the first match. During the 90 minutes, the most frequent chant heard from the stands was 'Hopp Schwitz!' Hitler's intentions had now surfaced, and the French knew that just as the Nazis had reoccupied the Rhineland in violation of the Treaty of Versailles, they could extend their expansionist aims to other neighbouring countries. They and anyone who supported them, like Mussolini's Italy, were the enemies to be defeated and against whom one had to cheer.

The referees appointed for the games between Germany and Switzerland were two of the officials who more than anyone else had impacted the brief history of the competition: Langenus and Eklind. Langenus had arbitrated the fiery final in 1930 and had managed the diatribes of the players of both teams on every little question – even on the choice of the ball, and then played one half with the Argentinean ball and one half with the Uruguayan one – and had expressly requested, given the tension around the final, a life insurance policy and the possibility of leaving that very evening on a boat made available to him. When he returned home safe and sound, he also went on to take charge of a 1934 World Cup match.

Eklind had angered the Austrians after not penalising the charge of the Italian strikers on Platzer in the scoring of the *Azzurri*'s goal. And a few days later he had directed the final.

Karl Rappan, the Swiss coach who boasted a past as a player with Austria Vienna and had been team-mates with

Sindelar, Mock, Viertl and Nausch, knew that the pre-match predictions were not in his favour. However, the result and the performance of his team in the first match had satisfied him so he had opted to go for the same formation as a few days before and expressed the same philosophy of the game, 'Le Verrou', a very defensive style compared to the football conceived by his compatriot Hugo Meisl. Herberger, on the other hand, had made six changes since the first match: in addition to leaving out Pesser, he had had to replace the injured Kitzinger and Gauchel with the expert Goldbrunnen and the young Bayern Munich rookie Jakob Streitle.

Eklind blew the whistle and the match began: it looked like the beginning of the *Anschlussspiel*, with the Germans who put their opponents in trouble. Their attitude paid off immediately with a goal from the Austrian Hahnemann – who had returned to his natural position – in the eighth minute. The lead was doubled a quarter of an hour later thanks to Lörtscher's own goal. Rappan understood that his defensive set-up had to make way for a more attacking system as the prospect of reaching the quarter-finals was getting further away.

Germany seemed to be satisfied so eased the pressure, which proved to be a big mistake. Switzerland got a goal back through Walashek a few minutes before Eklind whistled for the end of the first half. The stands came alive and the cheers for the Swiss were rekindled once again with the shout of 'Hopp Schwitz!'

The second half turned any predictions upside down after Abegglen's double and Bickel's goal meant the game ended 4-2 to Switzerland. Adding to the burning disappointment of the nine Austrian players present was that ten days later they saw the Italy team of Pozzo and Meazza celebrate their second consecutive World Cup win, despite the fact that the fans present for the final had been supporting their Hungarian opponents.

According to German newspapers, the main cause of the defeat was the relationship between the Austrian and German players; between two cultures too dissimilar to be integrated with each other. On an individual level, however, some people pointed the finger at Herberger's choices. The Parisian press defined the German style as a 'sophisticated but too slow work of art', adding that a slow player like Szepan was not suitable for that match. Johann Mock, referring to the amalgam between German and Austrian players, said at the end, 'When one of us advanced with the ball, he knew that the partner next to him wasn't the one he used to play with. We Viennese players felt like a foreign body next to the German players.'

## 5

AT THE end of the World Cup, the Austrian championship restarted, albeit in an amateur format. In addition, a name change had been imposed on some teams. Austria Vienna, for example, were renamed – albeit for only a few months – Sportklub Ostmark.

Austrian football entered a phase in which several of the Wunderteam talents had entered the latter phase of their careers, and many of them did not even seem motivated by the prospect of playing in an amateur league shaped according to the criteria of German football. On the other hand, some of the talents who were to enjoy enormous success in the war years and later years, such as Franz Binder or Wilhelm Hahnemann, emerged at that stage.

With the outbreak of the war, the Austrian championship was temporarily suspended but it would resume only a few months later, in October 1939. The NSRL – Nationalsozialistische Reichsbund für Leibesübungen, the National Socialist Reich League for Physical Activities – reorganised the championships within the Reich and established a final tournament between the winners of the different Gauligen which would determine the champion of Germany. Other changes made by the regime concerned minor bureaucratic hurdles to facilitate the transfer of players from one team to another and the possibility of forming

*Spielgemeinschaften*, i.e. mergers between teams. Those who had been called to arms had to wear the Wehrmacht emblem, the eagle, on the playing field.

Minor teams from Graz, Linz and other cities were introduced into the Gauliga Ostmark, but the attempt to weaken Viennese football was in vain as these clubs ended up occupying the last positions in the rankings. But what bothered the local public the most were other changes, of a structural nature: clubs with English names were Germanised, the playing fields were decorated with swastikas and before and after the matches the players had to gather on the sidelines and show the Nazi salute.

The resentment towards the Reich manifested itself among the Austrian population not only in sport, but also in fashion, cinema and cabaret.

The 1938/39 Austrian championship was won by Admira who consequently took part in the German inter-war championship. In the final, however, Admira were surprisingly humiliated 9-0 by Schalke 04 of Fritz Szepan and Ernst Kuzorra, thanks mainly to the five goals scored by Ernst Kalwitzki. Hundreds of thousands of Viennese fans had stayed connected to the radio to follow the commentary from the Berlin Olympic Stadium, and although there was no tangible evidence, the prevailing feeling among the Austrian public was that this result was influenced by non-sports reasons. At the end of the match, German newspapers showed for the first time a tone of superiority over the footballing rivalry between their country and Ostmark. *Reichssportblatt* wrote, 'Admira will have to carefully analyse the match and accept defeat as a fact.'

Meanwhile, more and more German and Austrian players were called upon to serve in the army. According to *Football Sonntag*, 17 players from Austria Vienna were recruited in

October 1939. Two of them were Josef Stroh and Karl Sesta, the latter joining the Wehrmacht in May of the same year, while Rapid had lost five out of 41 players so far. In any case, the Viennese players were almost exclusively employed in civilian positions or in roles that did not involve combat. Fritz Walter, who would fight on the Western Front first and then on the Eastern Front, claimed that from the end of 1940 the majority of German players had been called to the front. Everything suggested that during the first years of the war almost all Austrian players, having remained in the vicinity of Vienna, had the opportunity to take part in the games quite regularly.

With the beginning of the hostilities in both countries, a famine situation comparable to that of 1917–18 returned. Football, in such a context, took on a specific role: it cheered the civilian population by distracting them from the painful daily routine.

The popularity of football, therefore, remained almost intact even though the teams participating in the league had been stripped of several of their talents who had subsequently been assigned to barracks or army divisions.

Since Admira's defeat in 1939, the football rivalry between Austria and Germany had escalated further. There was no longer any match that was not accompanied by controversy over the referee's actions or alleged political influence. The tension was also palpable on the pitch with more and more frequent clashes between players and fans. In September 1940, 'anti-Prussian' brawls and demonstrations took place during the match between Austria Vienna and Schalke 04, and the following month the SS reported similar incidents in the match between Rapid Vienna and Fürth. Their bulletin read, 'There is no sporting event that involves a team from Ostmark and Altreich or even referees from Altreich that does not culminate without clashes or disgraceful scenes.'

Some newspapers were openly in favour of the regime while others were critical of directives coming from Germany. Football, in spite of everything, remained a world in which criticism of politics was, after all, accepted. Some newspapers, such as *Völkischer Beobachter*, expressed antithetical views on the subject in its various regional editions.

In November 1940 a friendly was held in Vienna between Admira and Schalke 04. Although the authorities intended it to be a reconciliation after the previous year's controversial final, the Viennese fans fed into the clash right from the start. The fact that the referee was Gerhard Schultz, who had been in charge for the 1939 final, had not helped to ease the mood. Schultz's refereeing was disputed: he disallowed two Admira goals and the match ended 1-1. A newspaper reported, 'The police rushed to quell the riot, seats and windows had been destroyed, the cops had been beaten and the limousine of District Chief Baldur Von Schirach was found with flat tyres and broken windows in front of the stadium. A sporting event was turned into a political event.'

Many decades later, that sense of pride and rebellion would remain in the memory of the Viennese people, although terms such as 'piefke' or 'Prussian', which were synonymous with Nazis at that point in history, would disappear.

Karl Stoiber, one of the Admira fans directly involved in the clashes, recalled the decision taken by the Viennese supporters, 'If we hadn't won the return game, we'd have destroyed everything and beat the piefkes. And when the game ended in a draw, we took the field and beat up everyone from Schalke 04, and before they left we threw things at their coaches.'

An Admira player, Karl Kowanz, also captured a positive facet of such events, 'Because of what happened, the piefkes no longer dared to interfere in this way when they came to Austria.'

The riots on the pitches continued. In fact, if possible, they were intensifying: while at first they had only taken place in Vienna, they were now also beginning to occur regularly in Germany.

Yet another chapter in the brief but intense rivalry between the Viennese and German teams was the final of the 1941 German championship, which saw Schalke 04 face SK Rapid. The match was scheduled for 22 June 1941, the day of the German attack on the Soviet Union. The beginning suggested a story identical to that of two years earlier, with a victory likely for the Germans. After only eight minutes Schalke 04 were ahead by two and after almost an hour of play they were 3-0 in front.

Within 11 minutes, however, between the 60th and 71st, the 95,000 spectators at the Olimpiastadion were stunned as Rapid drew level and then took the lead by scoring four goals, three of which came from Franz Binder. The match subsequently ended 4-3 in favour of the Viennese.

The reactions from the newspapers took on markedly different tones. While *Kicker* attributed the defeat of Schalke 04 to lack of luck, *Reichssportblatt* published a special edition through which it associated that success with the greatness of the Wunderteam, but was wary of mentioning the Jewish coach Hugo Meisl.

## 6

FOLLOWING THAT remarkable achievement, however, the Hüttelsdorfers collapsed. Eight of the starting line-up soon no longer wore the green-and-white shirt again, and during the next three years Viennese football would be dominated by another side, First Vienna. Rumours were circulating, and one of the prevailing thoughts that spread through the streets of Vienna was that in Altreich the victory of an Austrian team in the highest German competition had not exactly gone down well.

Moreover, the problem of clashes and riots in the stands remained unresolved. This had convinced Guido Von Mengden, director of the NSRL, to convene a meeting in Vienna with Baldur Von Schirach, Gauleiter – the head of the local section of the NSDAP.

Thomas Kozich, deputy mayor of Vienna, had repeatedly spoken out against the impositions that Viennese sport had had to endure. And following the various episodes between the fans, he reportedly published a report aimed at justifying the reactions of the Austrian public. Kozich's statements were widely debated during the meeting in Vienna, and Von Mengden justified such harassment by arguing that the development and success of Viennese sport had been largely promoted and financed by the local Jewish community.

Another issue on the spokesmen's notebooks was that of the calls to the front: Von Mengden observed how the Reichssportführer wanted the best athletes to be also the best soldiers, and that compared to other teams the SK Rapid players had been able to maintain their occupation.

But not long afterwards, some of SK Rapid's biggest stars including Franz Binder, Hans Pesser and Rudolf Raftl were recruited. At first they were all assigned to units and barracks based in and around Vienna.

Several Viennese and German newspapers reported on the recruitment of the players. Among them was *Kicker*, which carried a piece on 11 February 1941 entitled 'Radioman Binder'. Two editions later, *Kicker* also showed a picture of Binder eating in uniform and wrote, 'Binder also knows how to make snacks.' The fact that the Viennese players had the opportunity to stay in the vicinity of their home town meant that the Austrian league would remain effectively untouched. Binder was able to play without interruption until the end of the championship, and so did Raftl and Skoumal, except on one occasion. Pesser did not, but only because of a serious knee injury.

As was the case in Germany, clubs in Austria often tried to obtain permits for their players or at least required that they were not assigned to infantry or other positions involving combat and physical contact.

Over the years, however, it became increasingly difficult to get such favours, especially from June 1941, when the German army began marching on the Eastern Front. Binder began regular service, while Raftl, Pesser and Skoumal played very few matches during the 1941/42 season.

Like Rapid, Schalke 04, Dresdner and other German teams would have been weakened by the calls to the front in 1940 and 1941. In January 1942 the magazine *Fussbal* wrote,

'At Rapid and Dresdner exactly what happened to hundreds of other German clubs before them has happened, and no club will be spared in the future. The front has precedence over everything, and our sport also has to pay duty.'

It was a phase in which the Viennese football scene was drastically impoverished and the stadiums began to empty: international competitions no longer existed and most of the fans now served at the front. Results counted less and less. However, the matches continued until 1945, although it was not uncommon for players and spectators to go to the stadium and then discover that the match had been cancelled due to a bomb scare.

Contrary to other environments, such as cinemas, theatres and dance halls, which had long since been closed, the regime's opinion on sport was totally different. In a note it was said, 'All the most important military leaders agree that exercise is essential. The benefits of sport and exercise on people's health, productivity and attitude are evident.'

Some testimonies of athletes and coaches of the time seemed to refute the argument that football would not be affected by the decisions of the regime. WAC defender Otto Fodrek once said, 'Politics never played a role in football. Nobody ever told us anything about a party or other political issues.' Alfred Körner, Rapid's striker, believed that sport could not be influenced and said, 'On the football pitch there was truth.' Robert Dienst, a prolific Rapid striker in the following years and then only 15 years old, later recalled, 'People were quiet, nobody dared do or say anything, nobody. Especially not within the club. Our coach always told us, "Guys, this is none of our business. We play football, and we don't care about anything else."'

The fact that Austrian football under the Reich remained unconnected with political issues was also evidenced by the lack of police reports on stadium incidents. Hundreds of reports were filed on a daily basis about incidents in cafés, on transport or on the streets, but the world of football was unaffected.

On closer inspection, of all the promises of the regime, that of a weekly football match was the easiest to achieve compared to a Volkswagen, a house or household appliances. Otto Fodrek summed up the role of football in those years:

'We always got ready for the games a week in advance. We lived for the sport. Especially in my younger years, football was a mission and I felt it filled my life.'

# 7

MEANWHILE, THE absence of several players in Vienna had become apparent. At the end of 1942, Franz Binder was transferred to a paramedical unit and a few months later he was sent to the Eastern Front. This limited him to only sporadic appearances.

The calls to the front, together with the loss of some players as a result of the war, had revolutionised the team. Karl Gall, for example, of Austria Vienna and the Wunderteam, died in February 1943 on the Eastern Front, and the same fate befell his team-mate Franz Riegler exactly two years later following an Allied bombardment of Vienna. Rapid's forward August Fellner perished on the Western Front in December 1944, while Engelbert Uridil and Wilhelm Holec were reported missing in the summer of 1944 and February 1945 respectively.

However, the teams had been able to reconstitute themselves quite easily thanks to the acquisition of new players, the drafting of players from the youth groups and some returns from the front. These were, however, teams that had been shaken up, mainly consisting of players who were not available on a regular basis. Sometimes, as at the Viennese derby between FK Austria and Rapid in December 1942, FK Austria looked for players in the stands just before the start of the match.

Some players, such as Rudolf Raftl, Franz Kaspirek and Leopold Gernhardt, returned to Vienna in 1942. They were eventually joined by Alfred Körner, Ernst Happel and Franz Prak. Interviewed years later, Alfred Körner said, 'Rapid was able to make sure that its players were always just a stone's throw away.' In fact, this approach was shared with several clubs in the capital.

In addition, the Viennese players who had become part of the German national team could also count on the support of Reichstrainer Sepp Herberger. The coach, in an attempt to keep his athletes away from the war, undertook the so-called 'Operation Heldenklau', literally 'Operation Hero Theft'. So Herberger, although he was NSDAP affiliate number 2085548, created a list of 25 players who were supposed to return from the front, and this operation succeeded in almost all instances. In some cases, Herberger required permission for his players even for friendly matches, such as in January 1942 when he summoned Franz Wagner for a fixture in Zagreb, effectively removing him from the ranks of the Wehrmacht.

With the outbreak of war, military teams were formed whose ranks often included professional Austrian players. They also took part in the various regional Gauligen and Tschammerpokal. The most popular of these was LSV Markersdorf, which included top stars of the time such as Karl Sesta and Franz Riegler along with others from Admira and Rapid. Another of the most successful military teams was Roten Jäger, founded by Hermann Graf, in which Josef 'Pepi' Stroh and Admira player Franz Hanreitner played.

Those who remained at the front were often used for propaganda purposes. On 2 June 1943, *Völkischer Beobachter* published a picture of Franz Binder and an article about him: 'The good "Bimbo" still plays, although in another region and not with the regularity of the past. That he hasn't forgotten his old love, football, together with his ability to shoot and control the ball, can be clearly seen from a letter from the Eastern Front that will make his friends at Rapid happy, as well as all the Viennese football and the German football community.'

## 8

ONE OF the most common ploys used by Austrian footballers to escape the call to arms was self-mutilation, although this method led to very severe penalties for those who were discovered, such as death or imprisonment. According to National Socialist justice, this kind of subterfuge represented something that 'weakened military force'. Nevertheless, self-mutilation had become an extremely common practice. Sometimes the players damaged themselves, while in other cases they were seriously injured by an accomplice.

The latter was the case of Ernst Stojaspal, who in the years to come would be one of the most worthy successors to the Wunderteam group, finishing third in the 1954 World Cup. In the summer of 1944, Stojaspal had met former class-mate Karl Lauterbach, a communist and fervent opponent of the Nazi regime, at the Café Weber in Vienna. Lauterbach, who had a mutilated arm, had been relieved of his military duties and Stojaspal decided that it was appropriate to imitate him. At the end of June 1944, Stojaspal asked his friend to jump on his arm in order to break it. In front of a coroner, Stojaspal claimed that he had fallen down the stairs, but the excuse did not hold up. A sort of epidemic seemed to have broken out around these accidental injuries, and soon a series of investigations and subsequent trials began.

Public prosecutor Karl Everts and the Austrian judge Breitler sentenced Stojaspal to eight years' imprisonment, despite the defence of the lawyer Bruno Eckerl, who had become president of Austria Vienna a few years previously in place of Emanuel Schwarz. Worse still, Lauterbach was sentenced to death and executed in February 1945. Stojaspal remained in prison until the end of the war and was compensated by the Austrian Republic as a victim of the Reich. Austria Vienna attacker Walter Probst was luckier as his self-mutilation was never discovered. In an interview in 2006 he said, 'I had a doctor friend who gave me anaesthetic before he started hitting me repeatedly in the knee and meniscus and then ruptured my cruciate ligament.'

The incident was investigated but Probst was never convicted because of insufficient evidence.

Franz Binder's medical records also reported two suspicious notes: a cardiac anomaly in November 1942 and an appendectomy exactly one year later, when the player had already been sent to the Eastern Front. But a 2010 interview with Binder's son, Franz Binder Jr., seems to disprove these serious health problems. In fact, Franz Jr. did not remember any heart problems for his father, nor an appendectomy, and he recounted, 'The one who took care of his illness was the doctor at Rapid, who gave him a three-month leave. After that my father would be sent to France, not Russia. It was the only time he was really helped.'

Binder himself said, in a testimony at the end of the war, 'I returned to Vienna in November 1943, thanks to a permit. I had come back to have an appendectomy so I wouldn't have to go back to the front.'

Other Rapid players such as Raftl, Hofstätter and Knor also had an appendectomy during the war years, although they never incurred sanctions.

A separate case was that of Franz Konecny. Admitted in 1943 for a serious leg injury, Konecny pretended for months not to be cured even though he took part every Sunday in Admira's matches. At the end of the season, he was the top scorer and helped take his club back into the top division. The deception was successful thanks to an exchange of names: Konency used a namesake who was presented as Admira's striker, although this person had nothing to do with football. But it was actually the real Konecny who took the field. When the hoax surfaced, the doctor who discovered it was bribed with 15 free tickets to Admira's home games. Konecny had not been the only player to have assumed a double identity: to cover up these frequent deceptions, the stadium's tannoy announcer often failed to declare the names of team members.

9

THERE WERE also some Viennese players people thought were Nazis, and who became committed to denouncing such attempts at deception. Two examples were Rapid defender Fritz Durlach, born in 1916, and forward Georg Schors, Durlach's team-mate who scored in the 1941 final victory against Schalke 04.

Durlach had become a professional soldier, and in February 1945 he was assigned to army patrol service within the Viennese constituency. Durlach was assigned to search the hospitals for suspects so that they could be questioned. Very tough interrogations took place in what Durlach called 'the fun room', which was where he practised authentic methods of torture that would later be documented by an indictment against him in 1947. One document, about an alleged torture case read:

'In the interrogation room, Durlach pulled a rubber truncheon out of a box along with a wire cable. Durlach tied Josef K. and Dr. Leopold Dittrich ordered him to confess. Unanswered, Dr. Dittrich struck Josef in the face while Durlach and another soldier punched him left and right. At that point, Dittrich said, "Do what you want with him, kill him. I don't care," and he left. Durlach then began to beat Josef K. with a rubber truncheon. After each blow, Durlach asked Josef if he wanted to confess. Afterwards, Josef K. lost consciousness and regained consciousness by kicking. Only then did he confess.'

Shortly before the liberation of Vienna, Durlach turned to the alleged self-mutilator Josef D. and said, 'Don't believe we were defeated, we still have several hand grenades and revolvers in store to send you to the afterlife.'

After the end of the war, Durlach returned to play four times for Rapid before being identified by one of his victims. He was arrested and ended up in jail without being able to be a part of the first post-war Rapid championship, won that same year. He was given several favourable testimonies, such as that of First Vienna goalkeeper Stefan Ploc, for whom no ill-treatment had taken place at the barracks where Durlach served and which Ploc used to frequent.

# AUTHOR'S REFLECTIONS

AT THE end of the 1954 World Cup, Austria achieved their best finish in the history of the competition – which is still the case today. Their placing of third was even better than the fourth achieved by the Wunderteam 20 years previously. Their exit, however, had not been the same: in 1934 the Wunderteam could have won the world's top event but for a much-discussed semi-final against Italy; in 1954, Walter Nausch's side went out after a heavy 6-1 defeat against Germany. It was an emphatic result, not least because Austria had been among the favourites again and according to everybody's opinion the Wunderteam had churned out yet another generation of potential champions including players of the calibre of Ocwirk, Happel, Hanappi and Stojaspal.

Four years later, when Austria took part in the Swedish World Cup, any links to the now-deceased Wunderteam had disappeared. Nausch had left his position and was replaced by a Viennese football icon in Josef Argauer.

From that moment on, no one would have dared to put Austria alongside the favourites to win the World Cup or the European Championship. The success against Germany in 1978, which went down in history as the 'Miracle of Cordoba', would have been a great feat and little more, since Austria had already been eliminated from the competition.

However, some questions remain open: where does the Wunderteam fit into the history of the most popular sport in the world? For many, the Wunderteam was a forerunner of Hungary in 1954 and Holland between 1974 and 1978; an innovative team, capable of playing spectacular football but lacking that something extra in order to win a world title. On closer inspection, however, there are some important considerations. When the Wunderteam went to Italy for their first World Cup appearance in 1934, no one could have foreseen that the event would be their only appearance in the finals.

Already in 1936, Hugo Meisl had begun to shape a third Wunderteam. The first had been the one that won the 1931/32 International Cup and the second was defeated by Italy in the 1934 World Cup, then the third was the one that played in the 1954 World Cup in Switzerland. A project had already begun and that had found its first success in the International Cup, which was interrupted in 1938 because of the Anschluss. It was a different team than a few years previously, yes, but not necessarily weaker and had qualified for the 1938 World Cup after winning 2-1 against Latvia. Matthias Sindelar had practically disappeared from the radar, thanks to constant knee problems. Other players appeared in his place: Bican, Binder and Hahnemann, three of the strongest strikers of their generation who would have won as much with their clubs – if not more – than their predecessors. Bican – who in the year of the Anschluss won the Mitropa Cup as top scorer with Slavia Prague – had become an indispensable focal point for Meisl's formation and would probably have remained in Vienna if the political situation had not deteriorated. Binder, one of the most prolific strikers in the history of football and a winner of both Austrian and German titles, played alongside him from the moment his club, Rapid, began to participate in the Tschammerpokal and the German championship.

The partnership of Bican and Binder would not have been a problem in itself. Hugo Meisl had already experimented with this solution and Bican had taken Sindelar's place, covering the role known today as the false nine, and Binder acted as a real centre-forward, a role that in the 1934 World Cup had been covered by Schall. Hungary in 1954 played with a similar attack, with Hidegkuti acting as a false nine in support of Kocsis and Puskás as pure attackers. Moreover, the generation that had taken part in the 1934 World Cup was still quite young and most of them played a leading role four years later.

Austrian goalkeeper Platzer was 27 years old in 1938; defenders Sesta and Cisar were 32 and 29 respectively, and midfield pillars Smistik and Nausch were 32 and 31. It is quite clear that the Wunderteam would have had the opportunity to shine in that World Cup, despite a big loss that had actually occurred the year before it took place: the death of Hugo Meisl.

The competitive landscape had also changed in part: reigning champions Italy were joined in the final by a strengthened Hungary. Faithful to the traditions of central European football, Hungary had among their ranks names such as captain Gyorgy Sarosi, Újpest star Gyula Zsengeller, and young Ferenc Sas of MTK Budapest who would soon escape to South America. The 1934 finalists, Czechoslovakia, were back with players such as Plánička, Puč and Nejedlý. The competitiveness of these national teams is evident when one considers the results achieved in the Mitropa Cup: in 1937 the winner of the top club competition came from Hungary, Ferencváros, who a few months later acceded their crown to Czechoslovakia's Slavia Prague. Also taking part were a physical Germany side, without their Austrian components, and Brazil, the only South American side present.

On the field, Italy deserved their victory and confirmed themselves as the first power of world football in those years. They dominated the final and, despite the whistles every time their players displayed the fascist salute, more or less everyone had recognised the value of their achievements. The Wunderteam, however, would have been a fearsome rival and were capable of, unlike four years previously, challenging their historical rivals on neutral ground. But of course that is in the field of hypothesis. As of March of that same year, the Wunderteam had officially ceased to exist.

# CHRONOLOGY: THE WUNDERTEAM IN 11 ACTS

**1912:** The collaboration between Hugo Meisl and Jimmy Hogan begins at the Olympic Games in Stockholm.

**1914:** The Great War breaks out: the paths of Hugo Meisl and Jimmy Hogan separate.

**1919:** Hugo Meisl returns to coach the Austrian national team.

**1922:** Sporting relations between Austria and Italy are restored. The friendly match in Milan marks the beginning of a rivalry that will continue during the 1920s and '30s.

**1927:** The first edition of the International Cup and the Mitropa Cup take place, with the participation of the Austrian national team and the clubs of Vienna.

**1931:** After the 5-0 victory against Scotland, the Austrian national team becomes the Wunderteam for everyone.

**1932:** The Wunderteam win the second edition of the International Cup and are invited to London for a prestige friendly against the English national team.

**1934:** The Wunderteam finish fourth in the World Cup.

**1936:** The Wunderteam beat England 2-1 in Vienna.

**1937:** Hugo Meisl dies.

**1938:** Following the Anschluss, the Austrian national team breaks up. Several Wunderteam players join the German national team.

# ACKNOWLEDGEMENTS

THERE ARE several people who directly or indirectly collaborated in the writing of this book. The first person in order of time whom I must thank is undoubtedly Gianluca Iuorio of Urbone Publishing. This book was born from mine and Gianluca's idea to tell the story of the Wunderteam in a new, unpublished format to cover the whole team and not only its most famous names, Matthias Sindelar and Hugo Meisl.

So I embarked on a journey of knowledge and research which took me first to Frankfurt am Main and then to Vienna. In Frankfurt I was cordially received by Wolfgang Hafer, nephew of Hugo Meisl and a knowledgeable writer about the Wunderteam. Speaking with Wolfgang helped me considerably: Wolfgang, who in 2007 wrote a book about the life and career of his maternal grandfather, confirmed my thoughts about some false myths that still surround Sindelar, the Wunderteam and the war years. The availability of first-hand sources was of great help in writing the chapter on Meisl and beyond. I still remember a phrase of Wolfgang's from which in my opinion one should always start when analysing the facts of those years, both on a sporting and historical level, 'The truth is that in Austria, from the post-war years, people tried in every way to distance themselves from what happened during the years of the conflict, and precisely for that reason false or at least revisable myths proliferated.' And this is precisely the banana skin on which authors and bloggers have slipped over the years: to return a romantic and untrue image of a player – Sindelar – who became a hero without his knowledge and against his will. As it happened with Gianluca, the collaboration with Wolfgang would continue even when I returned to Milan, when the book was being defined.

After three days in Germany I went to Vienna where I wanted to visit in depth a city that had always attracted me, but this was no pleasure trip: the desire to visit the local museums was soon put behind the job I had to do, in this case to visit the stadiums and museums of the main teams of the city. So I visited the Rapideum, having the opportunity to delve deeply into the history of Rapid, the team from the Viennese suburbs, and a few days later I made a visit to the Generali Arena, today's Austria Vienna stadium in Favoriten, a few metres from the Altes Landgut stop. Its southern grandstand is dedicated to the memory of Matthias Sindelar. Here, the club's museum also houses a section dedicated to Hugo Meisl that Wolfgang had mentioned during our meeting a few days earlier.

As for the other historical teams in the capital, I did not have the same opportunity: I was convinced that I could visit the museum of First Vienna, but I was informed such a site still does not exist although the club is considering opening one in the future. Only a couple of days later, my trip was enriched by a fourth chapter, the third in the Austrian capital. When I had been at the Rapideum, the guide who had accompanied me during the tour had suggested I contact the author of one of the books – which also appears in the bibliography of this publication – on sale inside the megastore. I had not considered establishing contact with a writer in Vienna, but I already knew of the person in question as I had read one of his academic articles about Austrian football from the Anschluss at the end of the Second World War. I then contacted Georg Spitaler and was welcomed at the office of the VGA – Verein für Geschichte der ArbeiterInnenbewegung – only two days later, where I had the opportunity to have a conversation with one of the most knowledgeable historians about Austrian football.

As Georg and I chatted, I became more and more aware of how difficult it was to dig into the depths of history, even sporting history. It wasn't just the classic myths about Sindelar that had to be debunked, but also different side elements. One of the questions I asked Georg was about the end that some players had met at the conclusion of the war. In particular, I wanted to understand what had happened to Jerusalem and Zischek, two Jewish players from the Wunderteam. Georg interrupted me by saying that they weren't Jews, and that this was one of the many stories that, after being circulated online, had practically become truth for everyone.

Finally, heartfelt thanks also go to Andrea Araf, my brother, who was in charge of editing and revising the book, to Alisa Canzio, translator and collaborator, who supported me in the translation of several important sections from German, and to Dean Rockett, who patiently reviewed my translation.

# BIBLIOGRAPHY

## Books

Aguinaga, H. W. (2008). *Fussball als soziale Aufstiegs-und Integrationschance am Beispiel von Migrantenkindern in Wien*, Wien

Allinson, Mark. (2006). Reading the Dollfuss Years. *Austrian Studies*, 14, 337-348

Bolchover, D. (2017). *The Greatest Comeback: From Genocide To Football Glory*. La Vergne, UNITED STATES: Biteback Publishing

Bowman, William D.. (2011). Hakoah Vienna and the International Nature of Interwar Austrian Sports. *Central European History*, 44, No. 4, 642-668

Braun, H. (2013). Soccer Tactics as Science? On 'Scotch Professors', a Ukrainian Soccer Buddha, and a Catalonian Who Tries to Learn German. *Icon, 19*, 216-243

Brizzi, E. (2016). *Vincere o Morire. Gli Assi del Calcio in Camicia Nera 1926-1938.* : GLF Editori Laterza

Dietschy, P. (2011). Les avatars de l'équipe nationale: Football, nation et politique depuis la fin du 19 e siècle. *Vingtième Siècle. Revue D'histoire,* (111), 35-47

Forster, David, and George Spitaler. (2015). Viennese Football and the German Wehrmacht – Between "Duty" and Evasion. *Historical Social Research / Historische Sozialforschung*, 40, No. 4, 310-330

Fox, N. (2003). *The Jimmy Hogan Story*. Manchester: The Parrs Wood Press

Francka, C. (2016). *Matthias Sindelar. Una Historia de Fútbol, Nazismo y Misterios*. Buenos Aires: Librofutbol.com

Gerwarth, R. & Horne, J. (2011). Vectors of Violence: Paramilitarism in Europe after the Great War, 1917-1923. *The Journal of Modern History, 83* (3), 489-512

Gerwarth, R. & Manela, E. (2016). The Great War as a Global War: Imperial Conflict and the Reconfiguration of World Order, 1911-1923. *Diplomatic History, 38* (4), 786-800

Hachleitner, B., & Colpan, S. (2018). The Wunderteam, Painted in Oil: Insights of Images / Insights through Images in Sport Studies. *Historical Social Research / Historische Sozialforschung, 43*(2 (164)), 93-108

Hadas, M. (2016). Football and Social Identity: The case of Hungary in the Twentieth Century. *The Sports Historian, 20* (2), 43-66

Hafer, A. (2007). *Hugo Meisl oder: die Erfindung des moderner Fußballs*. Die Werkstatt Gmbh

Horak, R., & Maderthaner, W. (1996). A Culture of Urban Cosmopolitanism: Uridil and Sindelar as Viennese Coffee-House Heroes. *International Journal of the History of Sport*, 13(1), 139-155

Lanfranchi, P. (2004). La consommation du spectacle sportif. Une comparaison entre l'Allemagne, l'Italie et la France dans l'entre-deux-guerres. *Le Mouvement Social*, (206), 115-125

Marschik, M. (2006). Mitteleuropa: Politische Konzepte – sportliche Praxis. *Historical Social Research / Historische Sozialforschung, 31*(1 (115)), 88-108

Marschik, M. (2011). Austrian Sport and the Challenges of Its Recent Historiography. *Journal of Sport History, 38*(2), 189-198

Marschik, M. (2018). Depicting Hakoah. Images of a Zionist Sports Club in Interwar Vienna. *Historical Social Research / Historische Sozialforschung, 43*(2 (164)), 129-147

Marschik, Matthias. (1999). Between Manipulation and Resistance: Viennese Football in the Nazi Era. *Journal of Contemporary History*, 34, No.2, 215-229

Mello, N. (2017). *Quando il Calcio era Celeste. L'Uruguay degli Invincibili. La Prima Squadra che Dominò il Mondo.* Torino: Bradipo Libri

Molnar, G., Hungarian Football: A Socio-historical Overview. *Sport in History, 27* (2), 293-317

Puaux, François. (1988). Il y a Cinquante Ans, l'Anschluss. *Revue des Deux Mondes*, 42-51

Rimet, J., Leblond, R., & Rimet, Y. (2014). *Le journal de Jules Rimet: Le récit rare du fondateur de la Coupe du monde de football.* Paris: First

Roth, J. (2010). *La Marcia di Radetzky.* Milano: Gli Adelphi

Saccomano, E. (2016). *Le mystère Sindelar: Le footballeur qui défia Hitler.* Paris: Les Éditions de Paris-Max Chaleil

Spitaler, G. & Rosenberg, J. (2011). *Grün-weiss Unterm Hakenkreutz. Der Sportklub Rapid im Nationalsozialismus (1938-1945).* Wien: DOW

Spitaler, G., Forster, D. & Rosenberg, J. (2014). *Fußball unterm Hakenkreuz in der 'Ostmark'.* Wien: Die Werkstatt

Tomlinson, A., & Young, C. (2006). *German football: History, culture, society.* London: Routledge.

Urbanek, G. (2009). *Österreichs Deutschland-Komplex. Paradoxien in der österreichisch- deutschen Fußballmythologie.* Wien: Editorial LIT

Weisgram, W. (2011). *Im Inneren der Haut: Das Leben des Fußballspielers Matthias Sindelar.* Wien: Egoth-Verl

Wistrich, R. S. (1983). Karl Lueger and the Ambiguities of Viennese Antisemitism. *Jewish Social Studies, 45* (3/4), 251-262

Zweig, S. (2011). *The World of Yesterday.* London: Pushkin Press

Zwicker, S. (2011). Sport in the Czech and Slovak Republics and the Former Czechoslovakia and the Challenge of Its Historiography. *Journal of Sport History, 38*(3), 373-385

## Online Resources

http://www.pragerzeitung.cz/index.php/home/geschichte/21129-wo-die-ziegelboehmen-lebten

https://orf.at/stories/2276443/2275943/

https://www.geschichtewiki.wien.gv.at/Admira

https://www.geschichtewiki.wien.gv.at/Vienna_(Fu%C3%9Fballklub)

https://www.geschichtewiki.wien.gv.at/Rudolf_M%C3%BCtz

https://www.geschichtewiki.wien.gv.at/Kaffeehausfu%C3%9Fball

https://derstandard.at/2000081171960/Ausgefuchste-Taktikvariante-Nazideutschland-abgeriegelt

https://derstandard.at/2000077195812/80-Jahre-Anschlussspiel-Ein-letzter-Tanz-der-alten-Wiener

https://derstandard.at/1389860025936/Ocwirk-war-eine-
Erscheinung
https://derstandard.at/1259281053241/Ballesterer-Ein-
echter-Wiener-geht-nicht-unter
https://diepresse.com/home/politik/innenpolitik/
weltbisgestern/310937/Scheiberlspiel-und-

# INDEX [PEOPLE]

# INDEX [TEAMS]

UTE (Újpesti Torna
Egylet) 25, 31
Videnske Slavie 74
Vienna Cricket and Football
Club (o Cricketern) 16–17,
42, 44, 79, 95–96, 109, 114
Viktoria Zizkov 34
Vindobona (club calcistico
femminile) 117, 202
WAC (o Wiener AC) 203, 239
Wacker Wien 91, 117, 122,
158, 183
West Bromwich Albion 17

Wien (club calcistico
femminile) 75, 90–91,
117–118, 122, 158–159,
183, 202, 257, 259–260
Wiener Amateur Sportverein
(o Amateure) 44, 74, 82,
109, 154
Wiener Cricketer (o
Cricketern) 118
Wiener FC 1898 97
Wiener Sportklub 202
Wienerberg 72
Würzburger Kicker 111

# Also available at all good book stores

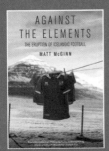

9781785317200

9781785317576

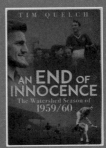

9781785317583

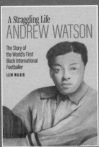

9781785318207

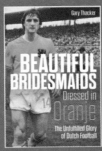

9781785318467

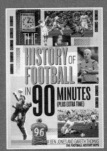

9781785318399

9781785317699

9781785318498

9781785314384